IMAGES
of America
NIAGARA FALLS
1850–2000

ON THE COVER: Honeymooning at Niagara Falls began in 1841 with a song called "Niagara." It was suggested that lovers could whisper sweet things to each other and not be heard by others because of the roar of the falls. Honeymooning peaked at the falls in the 1920s. The couple shown here in 1927 is standing on Stedman's Bluff, overlooking the Bridal Veil Falls, American Falls, and Luna Island. (Courtesy of Niagara Falls Public Library Local History Department.)

IMAGES
of America
NIAGARA FALLS
1850–2000

Paul Gromosiak
and Christopher Stoianoff

ARCADIA
PUBLISHING

Published by Arcadia Publishing
Charleston, South Carolina

Printed in the United States of America

Library of Congress Control Number: 2011943021

For all general information, please contact Arcadia Publishing:
Telephone 843-853-2070
Fax 843-853-0044
E-mail sales@arcadiapublishing.com
For customer service and orders:
Toll-Free 1-888-313-2665

Visit us on the Internet at www.arcadiapublishing.com

*To my parents, Christine and Dimo Stoianoff, and
also my Uncle Minnie and Aunt Joann*

—Christopher Stoianoff

*To my dear late brother John G. Gromosiak and
my nephews Tucker and Kellen Gromosiak*

—Paul Gromosiak

CONTENTS

ACKNOWLEDGMENTS

Niagara Falls: 1850–2000 would not have been possible without the assistance and guidance of many, especially Michelle Petrazzoulo, Linda Reinumagi, and the entire staff of the Niagara Falls Public Library. We would also like to thank Jim Neiss of the *Niagara Gazette*, the late Daniel M. Dumych for being a major inspiration, the late Orin Dunlap, Erin Vosgien of Arcadia Publishing for her guidance along the way, the Friends of the Local History Department, and all of the many people and voices that created the memories contained in this book. Unless otherwise noted, all photographs and images found in this book are from the amazing Niagara Falls Public Library Local History Department.

Thank you to all the local historians that are continuously helping me to learn and absorb the knowledge from the past. Thanks also to the leadership of Niagara Falls, especially Mayor Paul Dyster for giving me the privilege of being city historian.

I would also like personally thank the lovely Barbara Nichols for being awesome, patient, and understanding whenever I locked myself in the home office to type for hours on end and my friends and relatives who have always helped lend a hand whenever needed. Kelli, Leslie, Brianne, Matthew, Chloe, Gabbi, and Sophie, you get all my love. Another big thank you to Brooski for keeping my feet warm as I worked on the computer throughout the winter months.

Lastly, I would like to thank my coauthor and friend, Paul Gromosiak. It sure was fun to travel back in time with him.

—Christopher Stoianoff

This, my 10th book about Niagara Falls, would not have been possible without the help of my partner, Christopher Stoianoff, and the Local History Department of the Niagara Falls, New York, Public Library, represented by Linda Reinumagi and Michelle Petrazzoulo.

—Paul Gromosiak

INTRODUCTION

The Niagara Falls Public Library stands on a plot of land where Main Street and Portage Road meet in the heart of downtown Niagara Falls, New York. Much like the protagonist in *The Time Machine* by H.G. Wells, or by current pop-culture standards, Marty McFly in the *Back to the Future* trilogy, it is in this building that one can travel back in time. However, in this case, the vehicle that has the ability to transport you to the past is not a steam punk–style pod with twirling dials or a Delorean that relies on lightning power, it is a mere elevator that brings you from the first floor to the third floor. It is on this floor of the library that one can experience the Local History Department. In this wonderful portal, thousands of faces wait to be recognized and thousands of names await introduction.

It is in the Niagara Falls Public Library's Local History Department that Paul and I listened carefully to these voices from the past as they shared their stories for us to document in this book. *Niagara Falls: 1850–2000* is a celebration of Niagara's past, a whirlwind of images and factoids that will acquaint you with the "good ol' days" of our grand city. We have scoured through hundreds of photographs and documents to bring forth a comprehensive snapshot that truly conveys the nostalgia of our city's communities, neighbors, friends, and relatives. From civic leaders, politicians, teachers, clergy, and other remarkable figures in our city's history, including those that once walked on the land of Niagara and breathed in the mist from Niagara Falls, we have attempted to share a piece of each. Those that built businesses, raised families, studied in the schools, prayed in the churches, played in the parks—all who have helped the city grow and become as great as the natural wonder that perpetually cascades in our background.

From the first implementations of hydroelectric power, to the destructive power of the wrecking balls that brought down many of our city's historic buildings during urban renewal, to the majestic glory of the world's most famous waterfalls, to the smiling faces of the people who live and work within Niagara's roar, this book attempts to offer a glimpse of 150 years' worth of imagery that the City of Niagara Falls, New York, has brought to life. We have traveled down the gorge and onto the dangerous ice bridges, down many streets and into the neighborhoods and work places, through the entrances of some of the most popular restaurants and stores, up 20 flights to the top of the United Building and back down again to the brink of the falls, and below into the raging waters of the rapids.

Paul Gromosiak and I have written this book, in some sense a continuation of what the late Daniel M. Dumych started with his two books from Arcadia Publishing, *Niagara Falls* and *Niagara Falls: Volume II*, with hopes that we can affect someone's thinking the way he affected ours. We have observed his "visual echoes," and we hope that this book keeps those echoes traveling for years to come.

One

NIAGARA FALLS STATE PARK

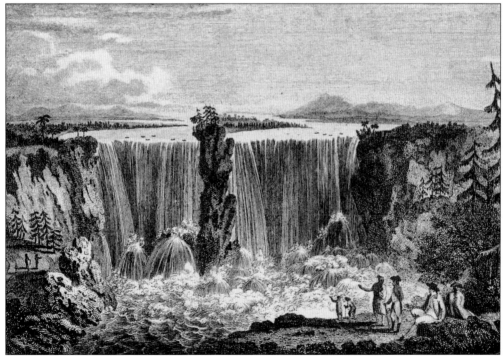

In 1678, Fr. Louis Hennepin became the first European to see Niagara Falls. When he returned to Europe, he commissioned this painting. Obviously, Hennepin's memory of the falls was very much exaggerated. He said the falls were 600 feet high and that the water pouring over them came from mountains in the distance.

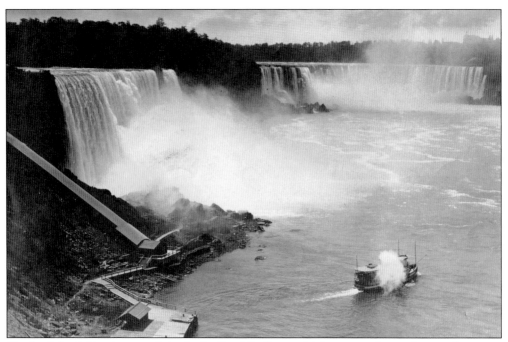

On the left of this photograph is the Inclined Railway, which once took people into the gorge. It replaced the stairway to the ferry in 1845. The Inclined Railway was powered by water. It was replaced by a pair of underground electric elevators in January 1910. One of the wooden *Maid of the Mist* boats is seen leaving its dock to take people up close to the Horseshoe Falls.

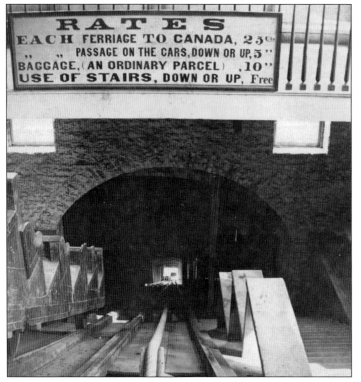

This 1874 photograph of the interior of the Inclined Railway shows the seats to the left. Note the sign indicating there was no charge to use the stairs. To get into the gorge at Prospect Point before 1845, stairs had to be used. Before the stairs, there was an "Indian ladder," which involved climbing down a tall tree using steps made from branches. Getting down was not much of a problem, but climbing up almost 200 feet was just the opposite.

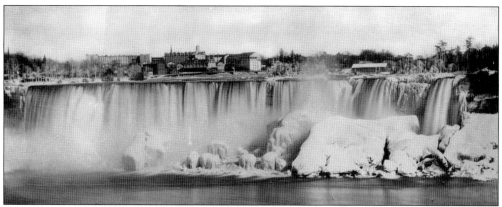

This view from the Canadian side of the falls and their surroundings explains why the Free Niagara Movement was created in the second half of the 19th century, resulting in public parks on both sides of the river. The American park was designed by the famous landscape architects Frederick Law Olmsted and Calvert Vaux. The International Hotel, the Cataract House, and Tugby's Bazaar are visible above the falls.

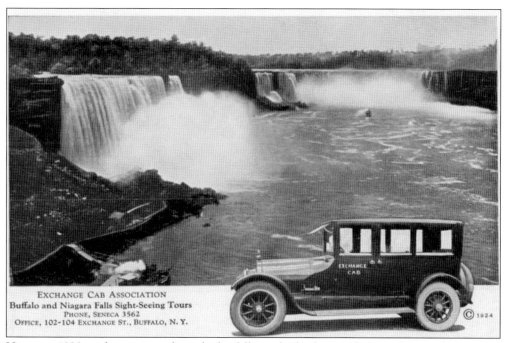

EXCHANGE CAB ASSOCIATION
Buffalo and Niagara Falls Sight-Seeing Tours
PHONE, SENECA 3562
OFFICE, 102-104 EXCHANGE ST., BUFFALO, N. Y.

© 1924

Here is a 1920s-style touring cab, with the falls in the background. According to the message on the back of the postcard, this was the "best way to thoroughly enjoy the splendors of Niagara Falls, with its many and varied points of natural and historical interest." Today, buses of all sizes provide a similar and popular business on both sides of the border.

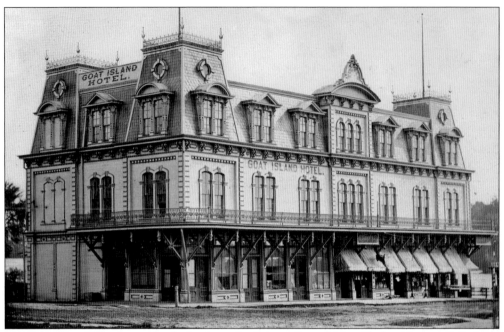

The Goat Island Hotel stood by the bridge to Bath (now Green) Island before Niagara Falls State Park was created. This was just one of the many places for tourists to stay while visiting Niagara Falls. The opening of Niagara Falls State Park in 1885 would displace many businesses in the name of beautification.

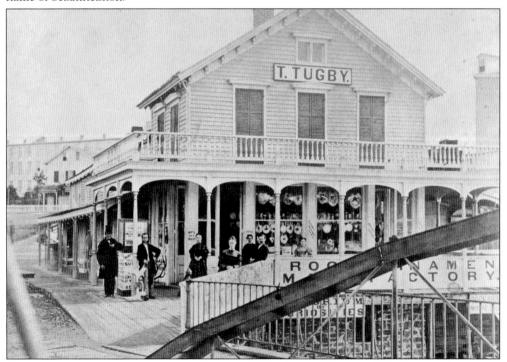

Tugby's Mammoth Bazaar is pictured here in 1885, the year Niagara Falls State Park opened. Tugby's was located just before the entrance to Goat Island.

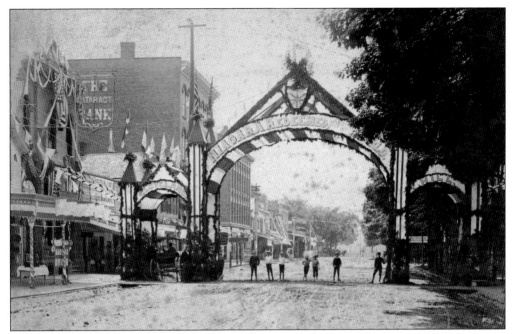

This photograph was taken from Niagara Falls State Park facing east towards Falls Street on July 15, 1885, the day the park opened. The entire city celebrated this event, closing all public buildings and businesses in order to attend the festivities. This park is now the oldest state park in the United States.

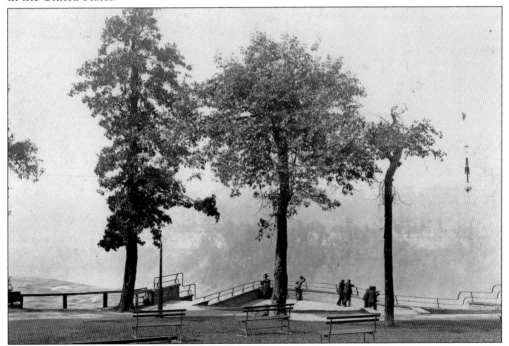

Here is a c. 1900 view of Prospect Point. The railings spanning the overlook were designed by Frederick Law Olmsted's associate Calvert Vaux. Prospect Point, until the rockfall there in 1954, projected out into the gorge many feet, allowing observers to look back at the American Falls.

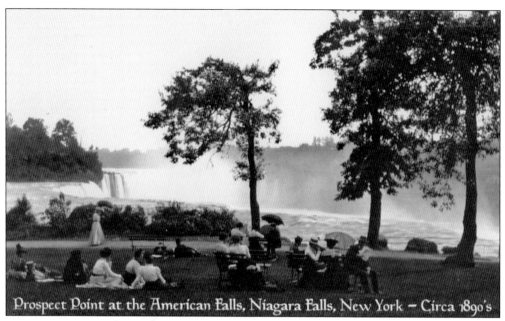

Prospect Point at the American Falls, Niagara Falls, New York – Circa 1890's

As seen in this postcard, the skyline of the Canadian side was devoid of buildings in the 1890s. This is a stark contrast to what is visible today.

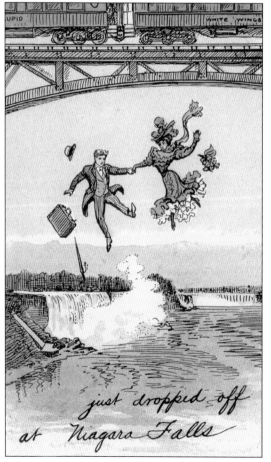

just dropped off at Niagara Falls

This couple appears to have jumped from a train going over the Michigan Railroad Bridge. The river is actually over 200 feet below the bridge. Humorous postcards like this were quite popular in the early 1900s.

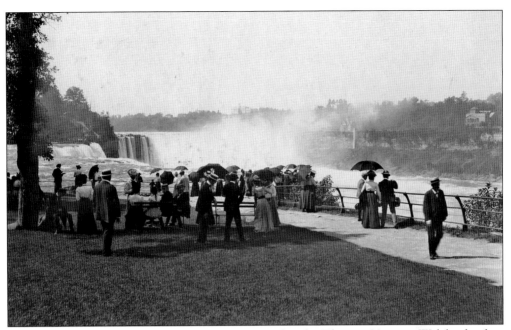

This c. 1900 photograph of Prospect Point was taken by Thomas Vincent Welch, the first superintendent of Niagara Falls State Park. He was also the assemblyman in Albany responsible for the creation of the park, the first public park in New York State.

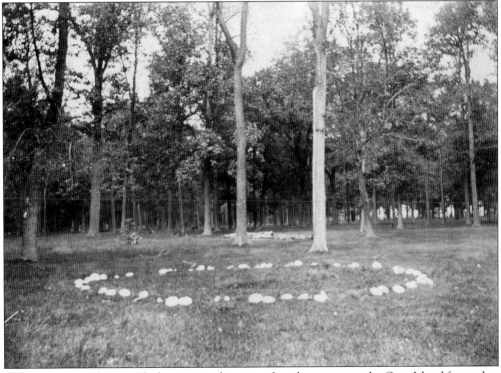

This early-1900s photograph shows a peculiar ring of mushrooms near the Goat Island forest that must have drawn the attention of those walking past.

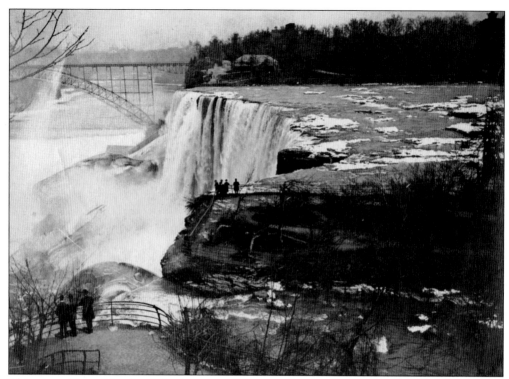

This view of Luna Island and the American Falls was taken standing on Goat Island in the spring of 1903. The building in the background is the entrance to the Inclined Railway. To the left of that is the Upper Steel Arch Bridge.

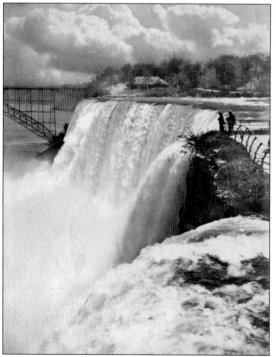

Someone ventured down the dangerous slope at Stedman's Bluff on Goat Island to take this photograph of the Bridal Veil Falls, American Falls, and Luna Island in 1910. Sometimes people risk their lives to get that "special" photograph. To this day, tourists on occasion fall into the gorge or go over one of the falls trying to get a better view.

The American Falls is framed by a nine-foot-wide Christmas wreath located at the *Maid of the Mist* dock on the Canadian side of the gorge. The wreath weighed over 70 pounds and was used for images on Christmas cards and postcards.

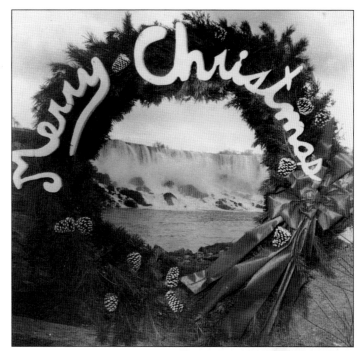

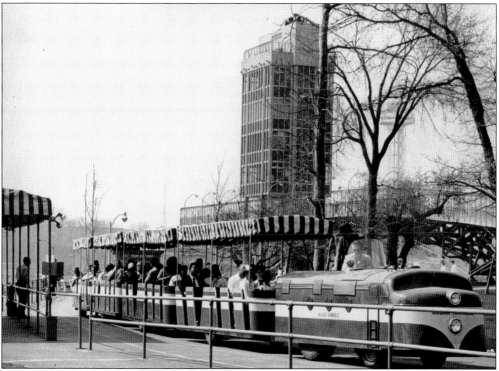

Viewmobiles transported people around the Niagara Falls State Park beginning in 1953. A jeep pulled three cars, and each car held 12 people. Musical horns provided a little bit of the first bars of "Cruising Down the River." In 1967, as shown in the photograph, the jeep was replaced by the "train engine." Today, trolleys provide the same service.

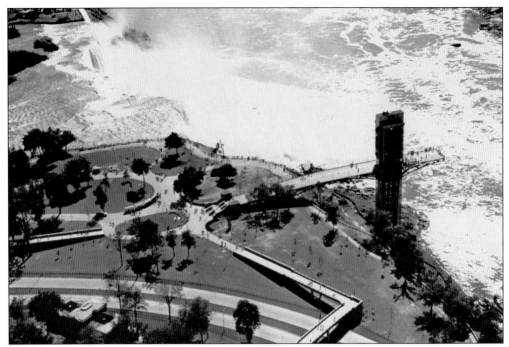

Here is an aerial view of Prospect Park (part of Niagara Falls State Park). In the upper left corner are the American and Bridal Veil Falls. To the right is the American Observation Tower with a deck for viewing the falls and elevators to take people into the gorge. This 1962 photograph shows the Robert Moses Parkway passing through the park. It was removed in the 1970s. In the center of the photograph is Prospect Point, a large section of which fell off in 1954.

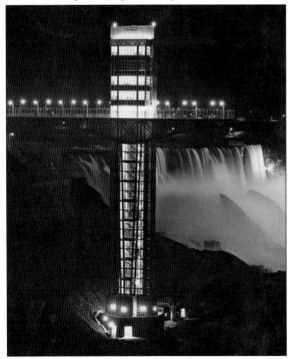

The American Observation Tower is shown illuminated at night in 1961, the year it opened. It was built to replace the underground elevators, which were ruined by groundwater before, during, and after the rockfall at Prospect Point in 1954.

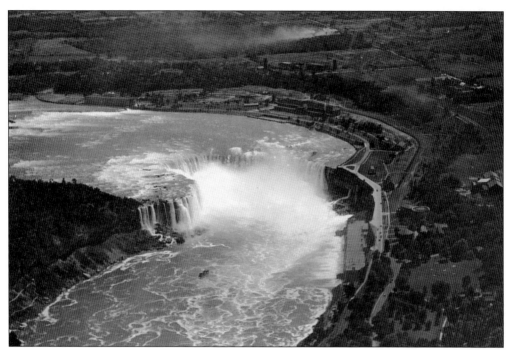

Horseshoe Rapids can clearly be seen going over the Horseshoe Falls in the early 1900s. Compared to today, the Canadian side is quite undeveloped. Massive hotels and casinos now dot much of the landscape to the right in this photograph.

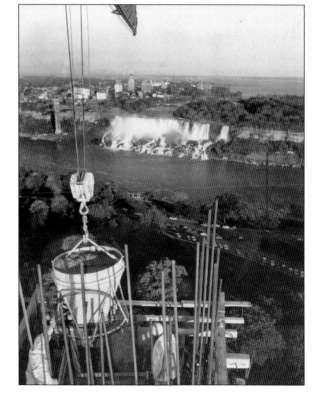

The Skylon Tower, under construction in this photograph, was opened in October 1965. It is 521 feet high and offers a great view of the Niagara Falls. This view from the 380-foot level shows the American and Bridal Veil Falls surrounded by Niagara Falls State Park. On the left in the background is the city of Niagara Falls, New York. In the upper right of the photograph is the Niagara River.

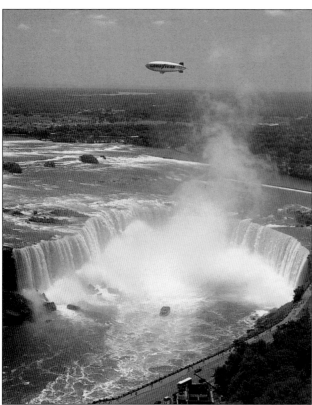

The Goodyear Blimp is pictured in the sky above the falls around 1980. It was once a common sight in the summer months. The *Maid of the Mist*, full of passengers enjoying a close-up view of the mighty falls, can be seen in the waters directly beneath the blimp.

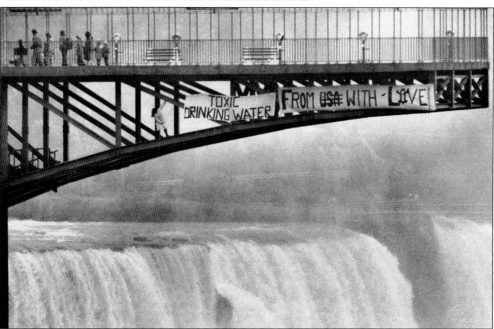

On Thursday, June 13, 1985, Greenpeace environmental activists demonstrated against pollution in the Niagara River by placing the banners shown here below the deck of the American Observation Tower in Niagara Falls State Park.

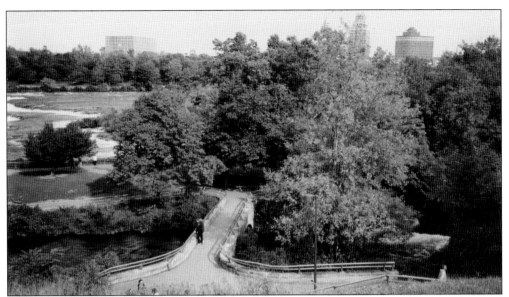

This is the bridge to Luna Island from Stedman's Bluff on Goat Island around 1985. In the background are, from left to right, the Oxy Building (also known as the Flashcube and now as OneNiagara), the United Office Building (now the Giacomo), and the Hotel Niagara.

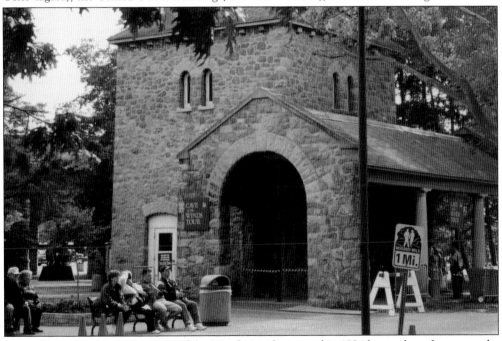

According to local lore, the Cave of the Winds was discovered in 1834 by two boys from a nearby village. A few days later, Joseph W. Ingraham, author of one of the first Niagara Falls guidebooks, entered the cave. From 1829 to 1926, to go from the top of Goat Island down to the cave, visitors used enclosed, wooden, Biddle stairs, named after Nicholas Biddle, the Philadelphia banker and financier who underwrote their construction. Shown here in 1999, the elevators in the rustic stone building replaced the stairs. Over time, the cave lost its ceiling, so the walk into it has become a walk by the Bridal Veil Falls.

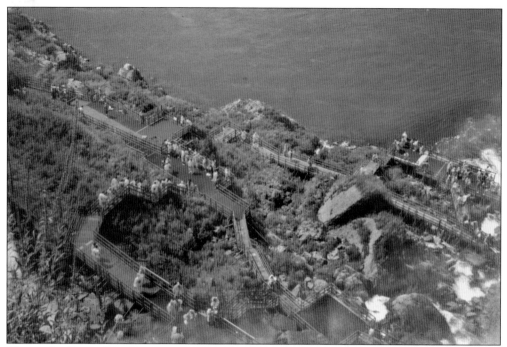

This is the Cave of the Winds walk as seen from Luna Island, the small island that divides the Bridal Veil Falls from the much larger American Falls. On the walk, it is possible to stand right in front of the Bridal Veil Falls on the Hurricane Deck.

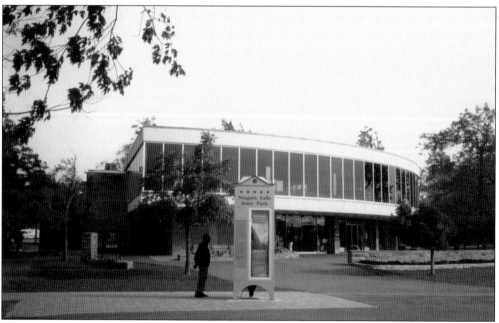

The Top of the Falls restaurant and gift shop overlooks the Horseshoe Falls on Goat Island in Niagara Falls State Park. The restaurant also hosts special meetings and social functions. The building was constructed in 1966.

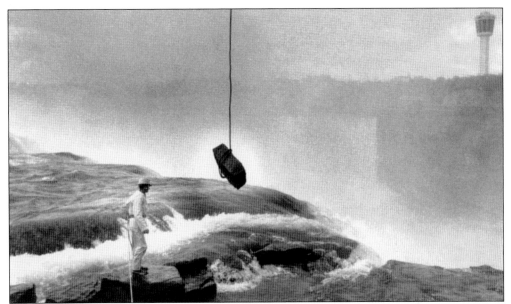

Much work was done in the second half of the 20th century to preserve an even flow of water over the entire crest line of the Horseshoe Falls. On May 25, 1983, this man positioned a large boulder at the top of the Horseshoe Falls at Terrapin Point. Workers were building a buffer dam to move a drill into place to make holes for explosives. This time, the purpose of the work at the top of the falls was to remove loose rocks at the point and make it more secure for the future.

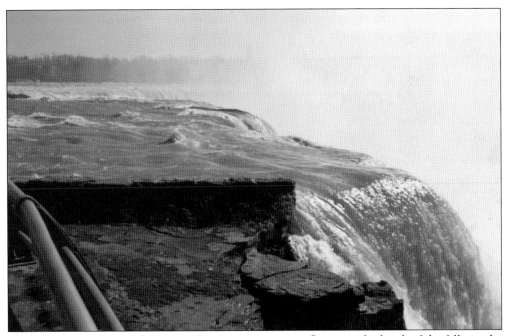

Note the erosion control device, used to promote an even flow over the brink of the falls, in the flank of the Horseshoe Falls by Terrapin Point. A lot of erosion control was done on the flanks during the 1950s.

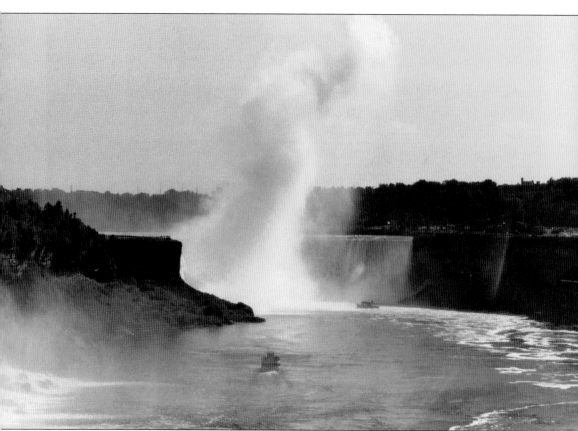

Mist by the falls forms in three ways. The highest mist forms when some of the water going over the falls evaporates, rises, cools, and then condenses in the air. Mist also forms when air just below the falls, compresses, rises up, and explodes, spraying the surroundings with tiny droplets of water. The third way that mist forms is the simplest. When the falling water strikes rocks or other water, it splashes, and many of the smallest droplets are carried by the updrafts of air produced by the falls. The Native Americans saw spirits in the mist—Heno, the Thunder Being, and the Maid of the Mist.

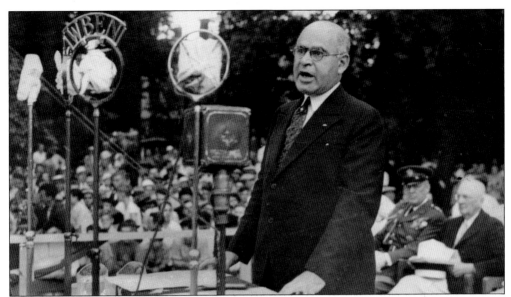

Gov. Herbert H. Lehman gives an address at the 50th anniversary of Niagara Falls State Park on July 15, 1935. Seated in the right corner is E.T. Williams, Niagara Falls historian. As a boy, Williams was present at the park's dedication on July 15, 1885. Born April 30, 1868, in the town of Somerset, he came to Niagara Falls in 1891 and worked for the *Suspension Bridge Journal*. He authored a two-volume history of Niagara County in 1921, amongst other works about Niagara Falls.

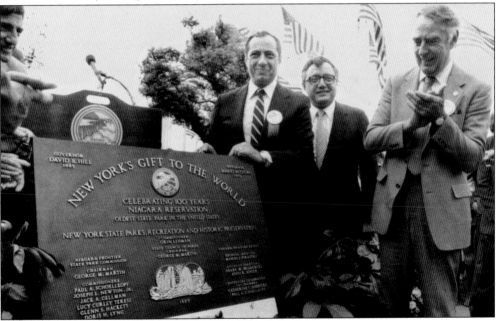

The rededication ceremony of the Niagara Reservation (Niagara Falls State Park) on July 15, 1985, took place at Prospect Point, close to the American Falls. Shown here are, from left to right, Gov. Mario Cuomo, Congressman John Lafalce, and Niagara Falls mayor Michael O'Laughlin. Before the rededication, a symposium on Frederick Law Olmsted, the designer of the park, was held in the Niagara Falls International Convention Center. The rededication was the highlight of yearlong events that included cultural festivals, concerts, art exhibits, and contests.

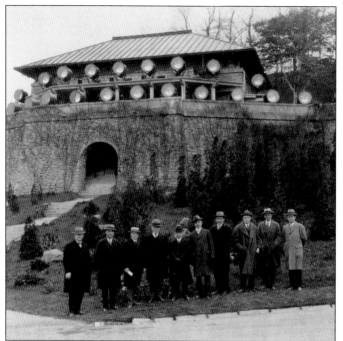

Members of the Niagara Falls Illumination Board stand in front of the new, permanent illumination battery in June 1925. The board was composed of 10 members, six from Niagara Falls, New York; two from Niagara Falls, Ontario; and two from the Ontario Park Commission. The battery was dedicated on June 8, 1925. Both falls were illuminated with 24 carbon arc lights, with a total of 1.32 billion candlepower. The cost of the lighting was shared among Niagara Falls, New York; Niagara Falls, Ontario; the Niagara Falls Queen Victoria Park Commission; and the Hydro Electric Power Commission.

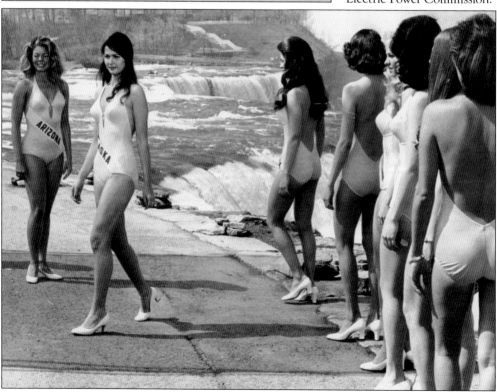

The Miss USA Pageant was held in the convention center in 1974, 1975, and 1976. Each of the three years, the contestants were paraded by the falls for photo opportunities by media and fans. (Courtesy of Ron Anderluh and *Niagara Gazette*.)

Roger Woodard, age seven, thanks *Maid of the Mist* captain Clifford Keech for rescuing him from the water below the Horseshoe Falls on Saturday, July 9, 1960. Roger, his older sister Deanne, and family friend James Honeycutt were in a boat that turned over in the Horseshoe Rapids. Honeycutt also went over the falls but died. Deanne was rescued near the brink of the falls at Terrapin Point by two men from New Jersey.

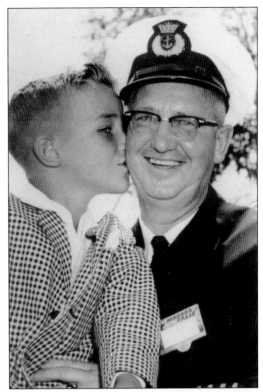

This was a more peaceful visit to Niagara Falls in 1980 for Roger Woodard. Here, he is discussing his accidental trip over the Horseshoe Falls with reporters.

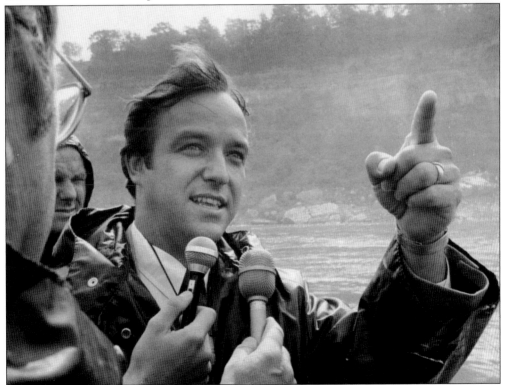

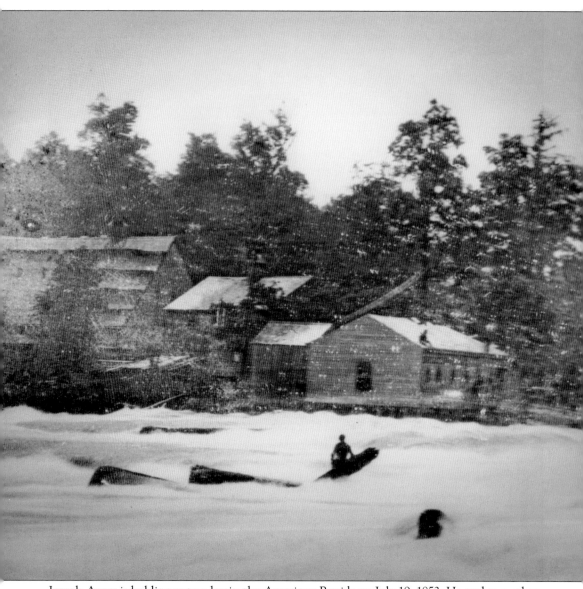

Joseph Avery is holding onto a log in the American Rapids on July 19, 1853. He and two others were in a boat that had turned over above the rapids. Only Avery was given more time to survive by clinging to the log. His companions quickly died in their plunge over the American Falls. Attempts to rescue Avery failed, and he, too, went over the falls to his death. The rock by the log that he clung to is now named after him.

Two

BRIDGES TO THE ISLANDS

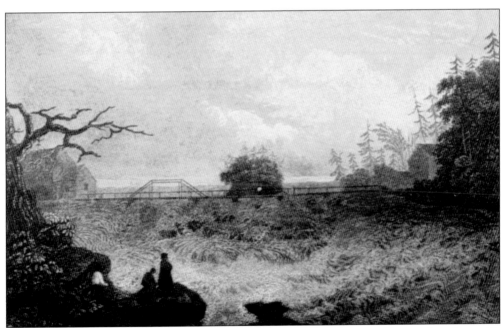

This is a drawing of the first bridge to Goat Island, built in 1817 by Augustus Porter, who, along with his brother Peter, owned the island. According to a contemporary of the Porter brothers, Samuel DeVeaux, the wooden span was built across the American Rapids in a laborious, time-consuming manner. The 12-foot-wide bridge did not last long, as it was destroyed by masses of ice.

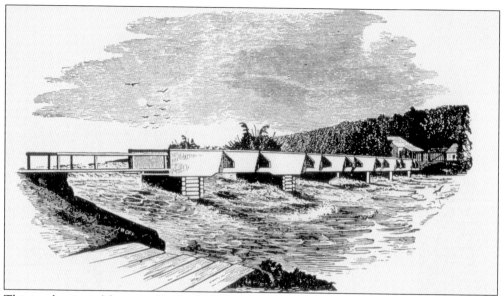

This is a drawing of the second bridge built from the mainland to Goat Island by Augustus Porter. There were two bridges, one from the mainland to Bath (now Green) Island and another from Bath Island to Goat Island. The bridges were wooden, replaced in 1856 by iron bridges.

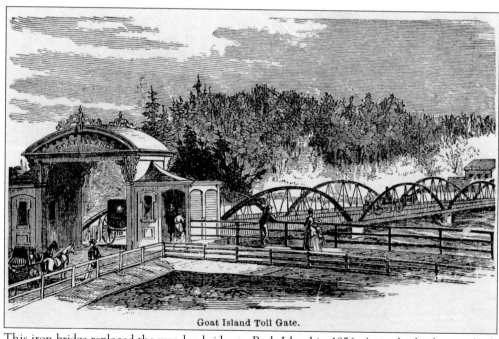

Goat Island Toll Gate.

This iron bridge replaced the wooden bridge to Bath Island in 1856. A similar bridge was built from Bath Island to Goat Island. Both bridges were about 990 feet above the American and Bridal Veil Falls. According to the *Niagara Falls Gazette* of September 24, 1856, this bridge was "another instance of the triumph of human ingenuity over the obstacles of nature."

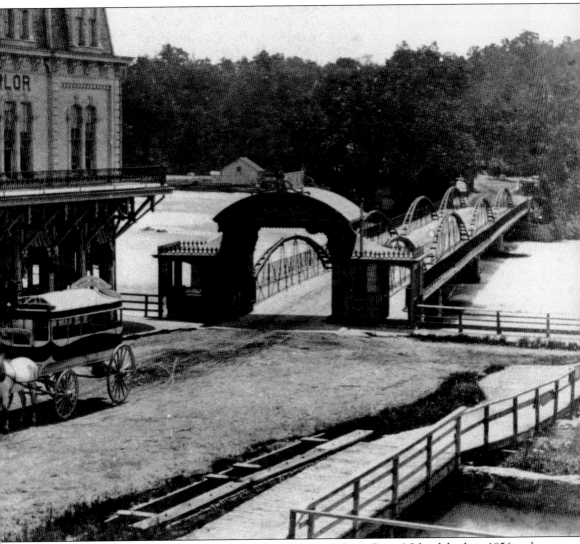

In the center of this photograph is the iron bridge to Bath (now Green) Island, built in 1856 and replaced by the stone arch bridge in 1901. To the left, a sightseeing carriage is parked in front of Tugby's Mammoth Bazaar. Note the building on Bath Island. Today, all the buildings that were once located on that island are gone, including a large paper mill.

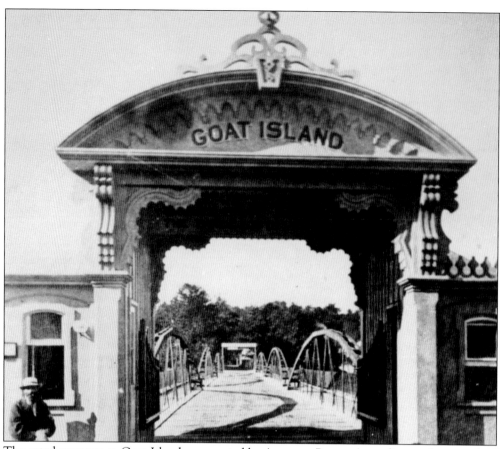

The gated entrance to Goat Island was erected by Augustus Porter. According to the records of the First Presbyterian Church in the village of Niagara Falls, Porter was excommunicated, having violated the Sabbath by accepting tolls on Sundays.

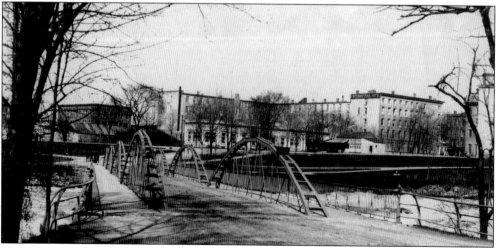

This is a view of the bridge to the mainland from Bath Island, after the creation of Niagara Falls State Park in 1885. Note Tugby's Mammoth Bazaar is now gone as well as all the buildings that once dominated the mainland shore. The International Hotel stands in the background.

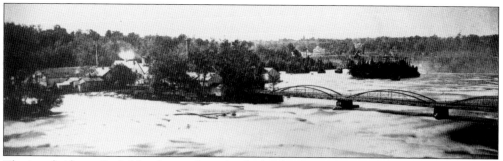

The iron bridge to Bath Island is on the right. Bath Island is to the left. The island was given its first name because it once had bathhouses on it, where tourists and local residents could bathe in the "curative" water of the rapids.

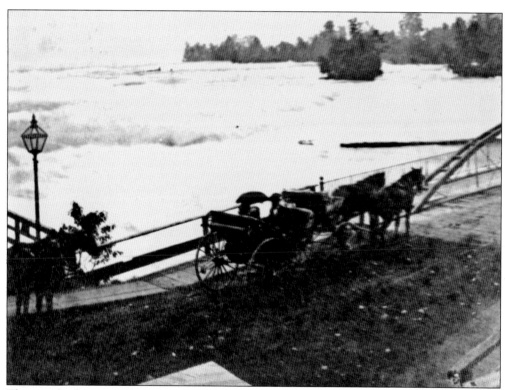

The iron bridges to Bath and Goat Islands were 27 feet wide, adding a double-carriage way of 16.5 feet, and two walkways, each a little over two feet wide. In the background is Goat Island. Pictured here from left to right, the two small islands in the front of Goat Island are known as Brig and Ship Islands. There were once small bridges connecting them to Goat Island.

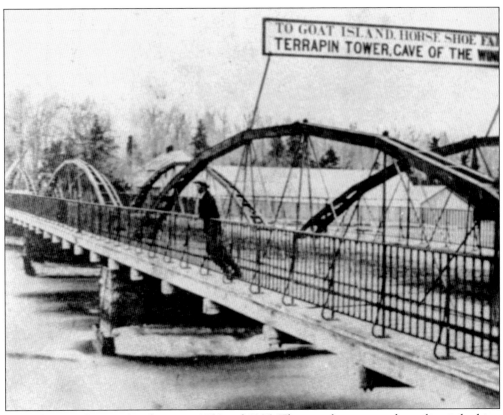

This photograph was taken between 1856 and 1885. The man leaning on the railing is looking upriver. People often lean on, sit on, or climb over railings in Niagara Falls State Park. Such actions are quite dangerous and can be fatal. The river above the falls, once entered, most often is fatal; a lucky few are rescued.

Before bridges were built to Luna Island, it could only be safely reached when the surrounding rapids froze. In 1821, C.C. Trowbridge from Detroit reached the island by climbing over the rapids on a low tree branch. The first bridges to Luna Island were made of wood and had to be replaced each winter. In the latter part of the 19th century, a more permanent bridge was erected. A lunar bow can be seen over the island on the night of a full moon.

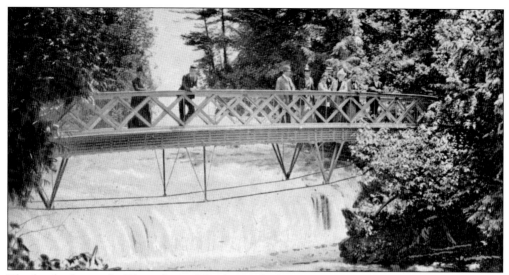

The first bridges to the Three Sisters Islands were built in 1868; they were suspension bridges. The one shown here connected Goat Island to the First Sister Island. The Hermit's Cascade, located below the bridge, was used for bathing from June 1829 to June 1831 by Francis Abbott. A young man from Plymouth, England, who lived near the falls, Abbott drowned swimming below the American Falls in June 1831. This bridge was replaced by today's stone bridge in 1898.

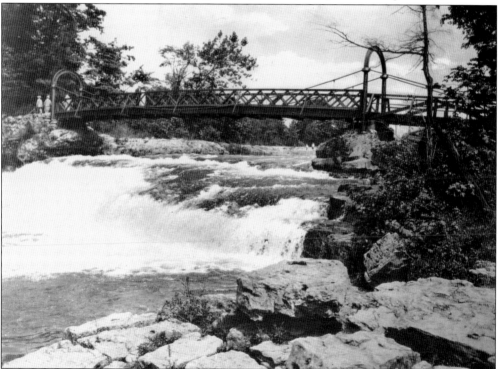

This suspension bridge connected the Second and Third Sister Islands, replaced by concrete bridges in the 1950s, along with the one connecting First and Second Sister Islands. The link from one of the cables of this bridge is still attached to a boulder on the Third Sister Island. There is an awesome view of the Horseshoe Rapids from the Third Sister Island.

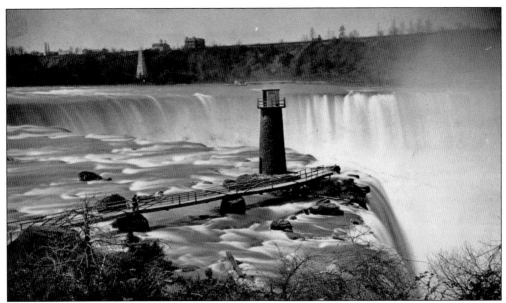

The stone tower is pictured here around 1870. Until 1954, Terrapin Point was known as Terrapin Rocks and was part of the Horseshoe Falls. The first bridge over the Terrapin Rocks was built by Augustus Porter. In 1833, Porter used stones from the vicinity of the falls to erect this 45-foot tower. It became known as Terrapin Tower and Lovers' Tower.

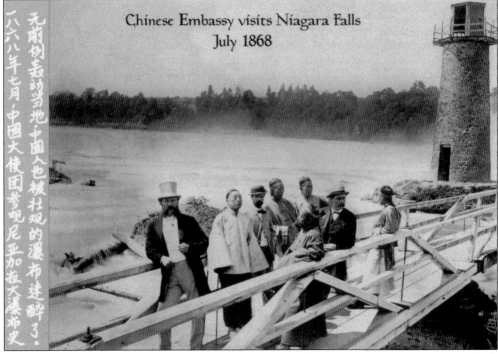

Nearly every year, the bridge over Terrapin Rocks had to be repaired and sometimes rebuilt because of winter ice damage. Francis Abbott, the "Hermit of Niagara," used to go to the end of the 10-foot extension of the bridge and do chin-ups, frightening women. Because of its poor condition, the tower was blown up with dynamite in 1873.

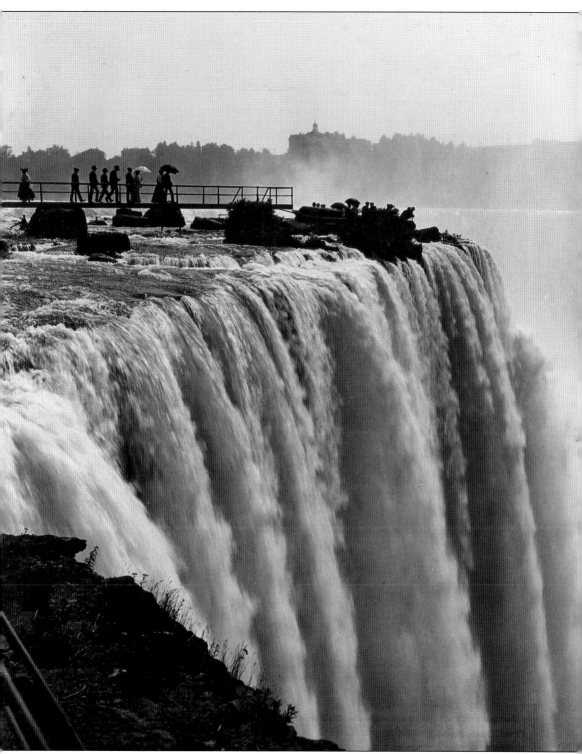
Terrapin Rocks is pictured here around 1900, without the stone tower. Today, this whole section of the Horseshoe Falls is dry, except for some groundwater coming out into the gorge.

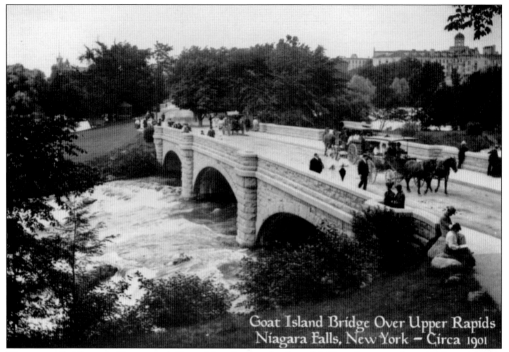

The stone bridges to Green and Goat Islands were built in 1901 and repaired in 1913 and 1966. In the right background is the Cataract House Hotel, once the most important hotel in Niagara Falls, New York. The stone bridges were replaced the iron bridges in 1856. The view here is from Goat Island to Green Island.

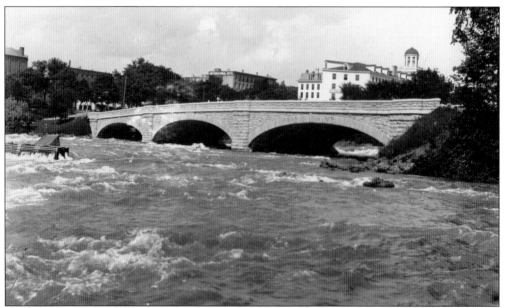

This is a view of the stone bridge connecting Green Island and the mainland. In the background are two of the most famous hotels in the history of Niagara Falls, New York—the International (center) and the Cataract House (right of center). The International was destroyed by fire on January 3, 1918. The Cataract House was also destroyed by fire on October 14, 1945.

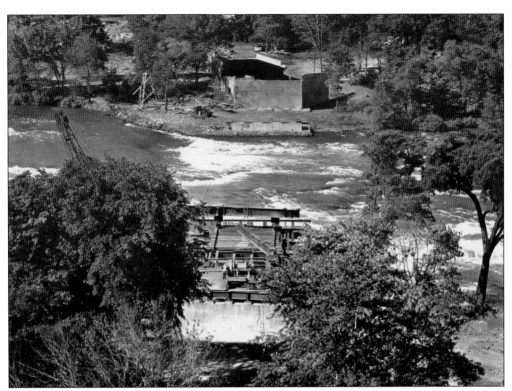

The start of the construction of the American Rapids Bridge is pictured here in 1959. This was the same location as the first bridge to the island built by Augustus Porter in 1817. This is the view from Goat Island.

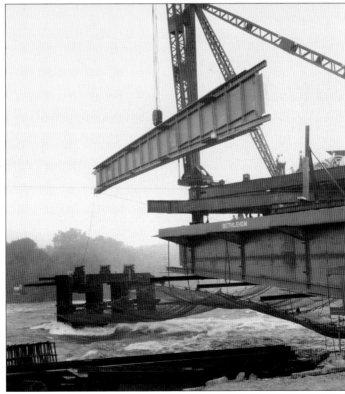

Construction continues on the American Rapids Bridge in 1959. At 590 feet, it was the longest plate girder bridge in the United States. It is about 2,000 feet above the American Falls. From either side are wonderful views of the American Rapids.

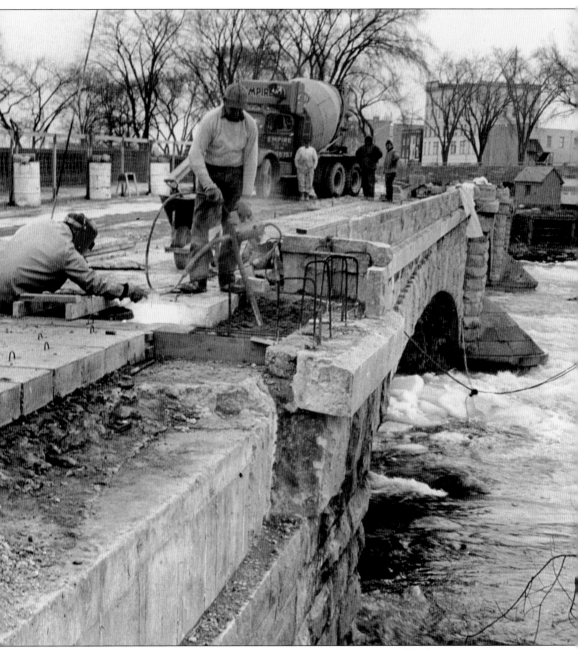

On April 11, 1966, the stone bridge from the mainland to Green Island was in the process of being widened and given a face-lift, which included widening the sidewalks, rebuilding the road surface, and adding new stone and aluminum railings. From 1900 to 1960, this bridge, along with the one connecting Green and Goat Islands, carried both cars and pedestrians. After 1960, all cars and other vehicles have been using the American Rapids Bridge.

Three

THE NIAGARA RIVER GORGE

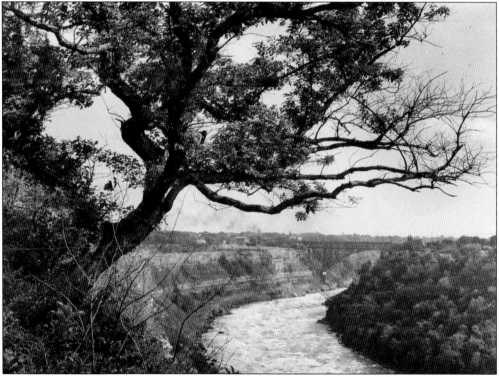

This photograph shows the Whirlpool Rapids to the south. The United States is on the left side of the gorge. The two bridges over the gorge are the Whirlpool Rapids Bridge and the Michigan Railroad Bridge. The large building in the middle of the photograph is the Customs House, built in 1863. It has been converted into an interpretive center of the Underground Railroad.

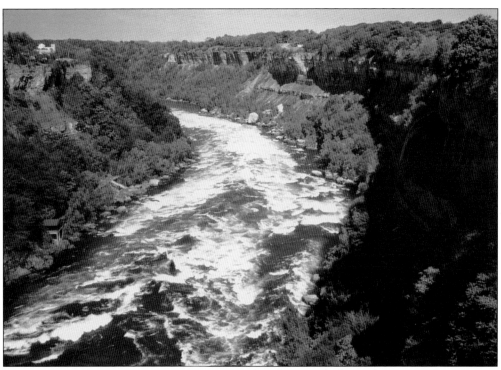

This photograph shows the spectacular Whirlpool Rapids from the Whirlpool Rapids Bridge. These rapids have been challenged by swimmers, boaters, rafters, and barrel riders, many of whom paid with their lives. These waters end in a mysterious whirlpool, which legends often claimed was bottomless and laden with gold.

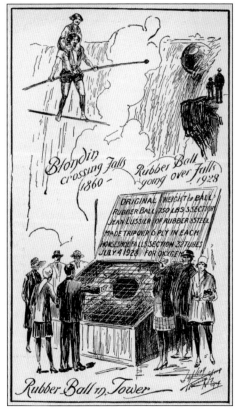

Jean Lussier's rubber and steel ball is displayed in this sketch on a postcard from 1930. The drawing of Blondin with his manager on his back shows them close to the Horseshoe Falls, but Blondin never had a rope close to any of the three Niagara Falls. Stunters of all sorts have found their way to Niagara Falls over the years . . . most were successful, a few were not.

Charles Gaskill's flour mill is shown around 1875 on the brink of the gorge, making use of the water from the hydraulic canal. It was the first mill at the top of the gorge. Soon after, this landscape would be crowded with industry.

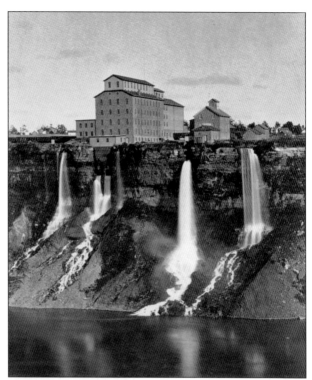

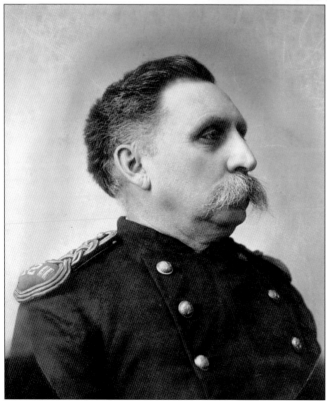

Charles B. Gaskill was the first investor to make use of the hydraulic canal bringing water from the Niagara River above the falls to the rim of the gorge just north of the American Falls. There, in 1875, he opened a gristmill. Later, Gaskill became the first president of the Niagara Falls Power Company. Today, there is a preparatory school in the city of Niagara Falls named after him. He is often called Col. Charles B. Gaskill because of his service in the Civil War and Spanish–American War.

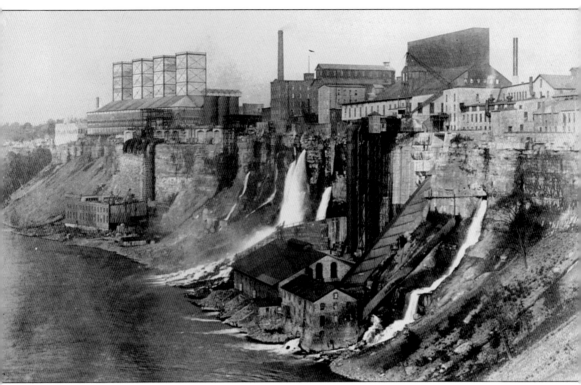

Part of the mill district in Niagara Falls, New York, is at the top of this c. 1895 photograph. To the far left is the Aluminum Company of America (ALCOA). In the bottom of the gorge are two hydroelectric power plants owned by the Hydraulic Power and Manufacturing Company.

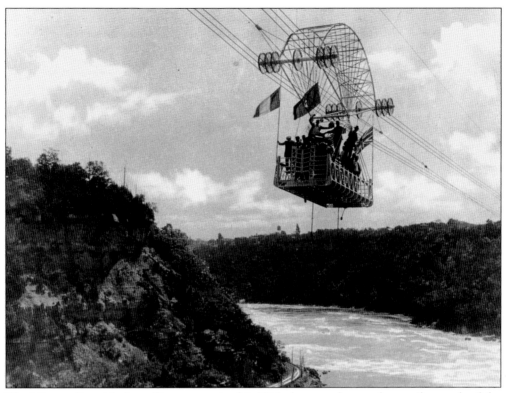

The Niagara Spanish Aero Car, as seen in this 1916 photograph, was three miles north of the falls. St. David's Gorge, around the whirlpool, was buried during the Ice Age and partially cleaned out when the present gorge was being made about 4,000 years ago.

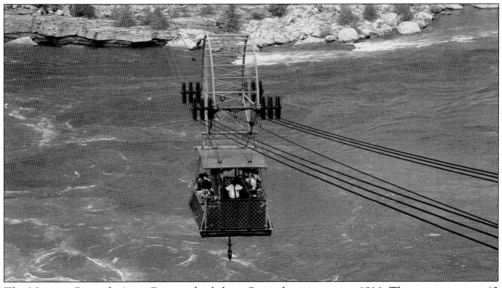

The Niagara Spanish Aero Car was built by a Spanish company in 1916. The car can carry 40 people standing, and it takes about five minutes to cross the whirlpool. Seen here in the 1980s, it had been renovated and modernized. The carriage and cable system is similar to one used at Mount Ulia in San Sebastian, Spain.

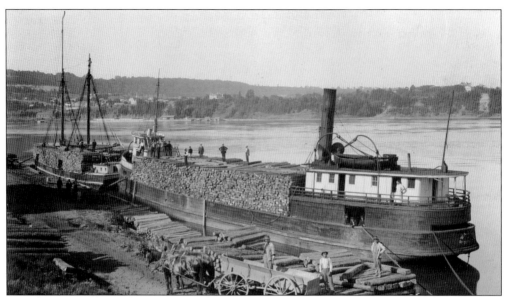

The Lewiston Dock is shown around 1890. The ship is unloading rail ties for the Great Gorge Route Railroad.

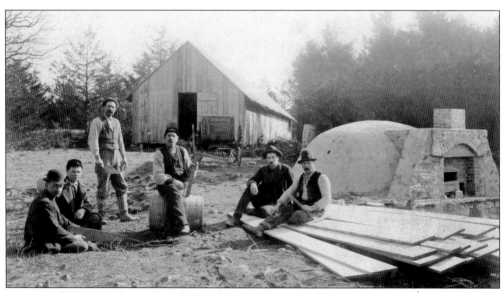

A group of Italian workers relax after working on the Great Gorge Route Railroad in 1893. The domed object to the right is a baking oven. Camps like these were common along the construction area of the Great Gorge Route. Workers from all over the world found employment working on the Great Gorge Route.

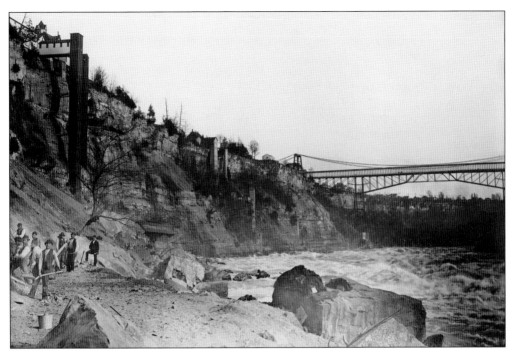

The Great Gorge Route operated in the gorge from 1895 to 1935. This 1893 photograph shows the work being done along the base of the gorge wall. Note the railroad suspension bridge and cantilever bridge in the background. The Buttery Elevators are on the left, above the workmen; they transported people into and out of the gorge by the Whirlpool Rapids. Frequent rockfalls and the Great Depression put the company out of business.

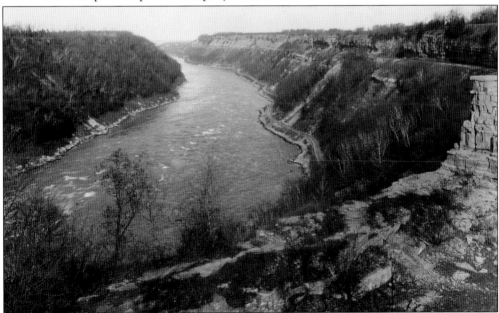

Note the Great Gorge Route tracks at the bottom of the gorge on the right side. This view is from near Devil's Hole, looking north to Lewiston. Today, the Robert Moses Power Plant is on the right side of the gorge; on the left are Sir Adam Beck's No. 1 and No. 2 Power Plants.

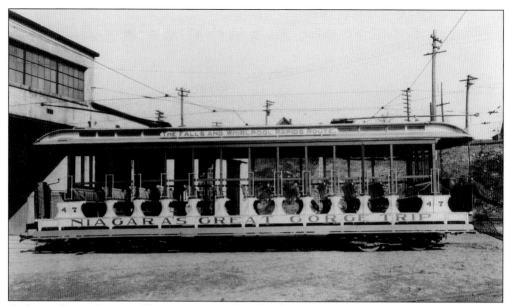

A Great Gorge Route trolley car sits outside of its barn on Spruce Avenue around 1915. On July 1, 1917, a car similar to this one turned upside down in the river about 50 feet south of the cantilever bridge. Ten people were killed.

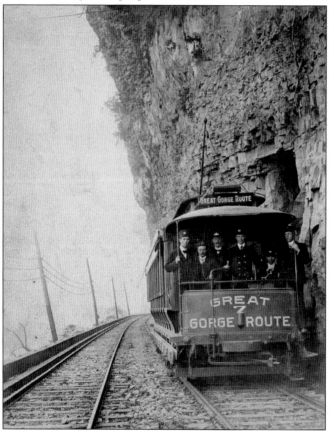

The Great Gorge Route was somewhat a risky ride. Rockfalls ranged from minor to major; some resulting in injuries and fatalities. The most dangerous time of the year on the route was the early spring. Water thawing and freezing in cracks produced sudden movements of rocks. A rock slide and the Great Depression put an end to traveling on the Great Gorge in 1935.

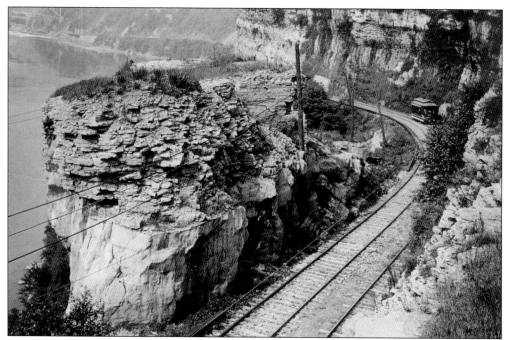

The Great Gorge Route took people through the bottom of the Niagara Gorge on the American side and along the top of the gorge on the Canadian side. This photograph was taken in 1911. In 1902, searchlight expeditions began. The night trips became quite popular. The first searchlight tour in the gorge was actually done the year before by Thomas A. Edison.

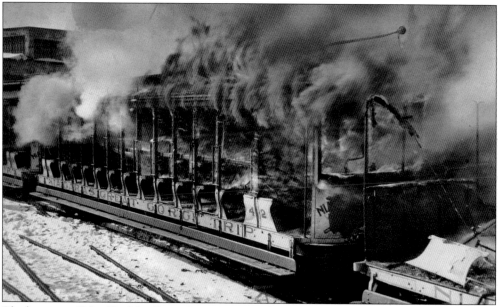

The burning of No. 42 of the Great Gorge Route trolley cars took place around 1935. Not a single car was saved. The costs of accidents and constant rock slides took their toll on the Great Gorge Route, which ceased operations in 1935. Remnants of the route can still be seen at the base of the Niagara Gorge today, but it has otherwise disappeared due to rock slides and nature growing over what is left of the platforms.

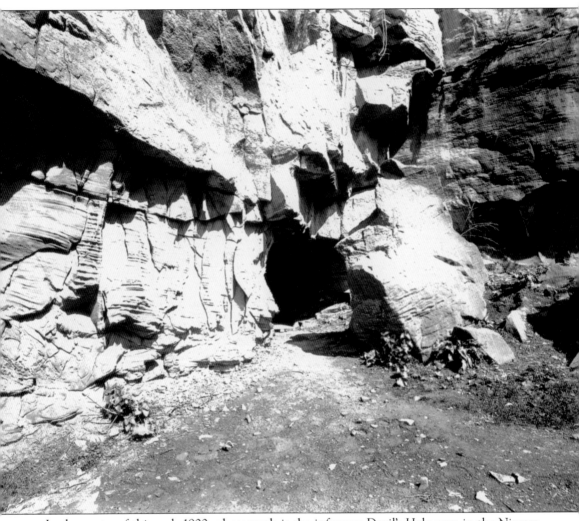

In the center of this early-1900s photograph is the infamous Devil's Hole cave in the Niagara Gorge, a few miles north of the Niagara Falls. Once used by snakes to hibernate through the winter, it later became the subject of legend, located near the site of a terrible ambush. The Native Americans had a legend about an evil serpent that lived in the cave; to enter the cave was to be cursed by the serpent. The French explorer LaSalle supposedly was a victim of the curse after entering the cave.

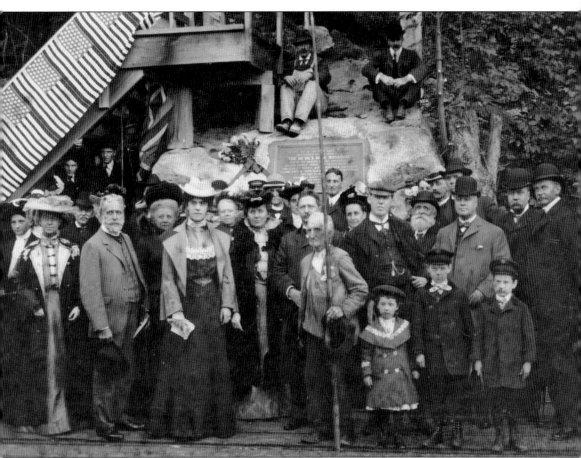

This group gathered at the Devil's Hole Station of the Great Gorge Route on Saturday, September 13, 1902, to dedicate the bronze tablet marking the location of the massacre of British soldiers by Seneca warriors September 14, 1763. In reality, the attack took place at the top of the gorge. The tablet was donated by the Frontier Landmarks Association, which had it embedded in a large boulder. The tablet bore the following inscription: "At the top of the cliff above this spot September 14, 1763 occurred The Devil's Hole Massacre when 500 Seneca Indians ambushed a British supply train, massacred its escort and hurled bodies and wagons into the chasm below. Only 3, John Stedman, William Matthews and one other escaping. Erected by Niagara Gorge Railroad Company and presented to Niagara Frontier Landmarks Association, 1902."

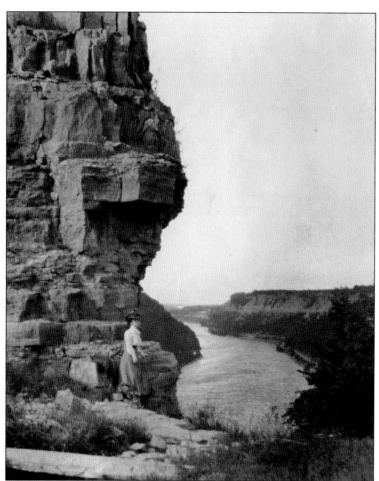

In the early 1900s, a woman poses at Pulpit's Rock, located near Devil's Hole cave.

These men, possibly on break from studies at Niagara University, are climbing to the top of Pulpit's Rock in the early 1900s. The university's buildings can be seen in the background to the left. Pulpit's Rock was blasted away when the road to the power plant was constructed in the 1960s.

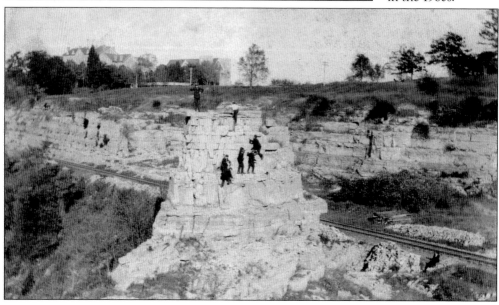

Four

BRIDGES ACROSS
THE GORGE

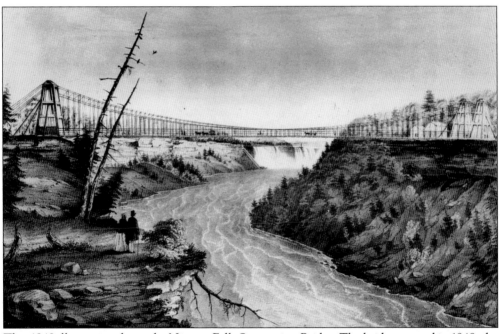

This 1848 illustration shows the Niagara Falls Suspension Bridge. The bridge opened in 1848, the same year Mother Nature nearly turned off the falls for a day. This was the first bridge to span the gorge. The bridge was perched 280 feet above the water and weighed 75 tons. It all started with a kite-flying contest won by a young American teenager, Homan Walsh. With the aid of the westerly spring wind, the string of Homan's kite carried the first cables across the gorge on his second try. His prize was $10 (some historians say $5).

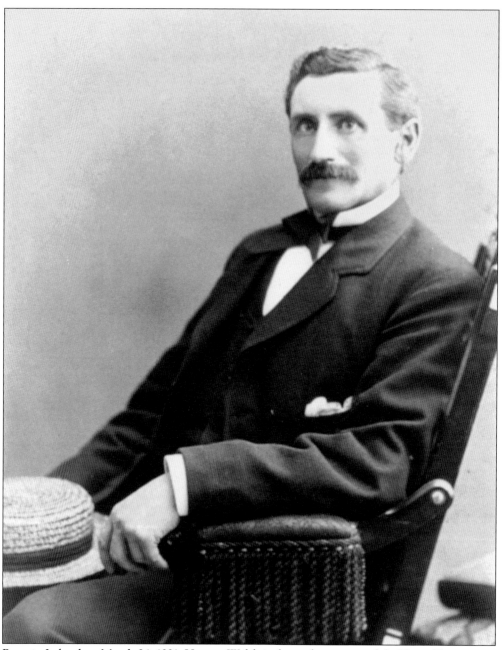

Born in Ireland on March 24, 1831, Homan Walsh is shown here as an adult. He and his parents came to the United States in 1834 and settled in Niagara Falls in 1840. He went on to become president of a bank in Lincoln, Nebraska, where he died in 1899. His body was brought back to Niagara Falls and buried in Oakwood Cemetery.

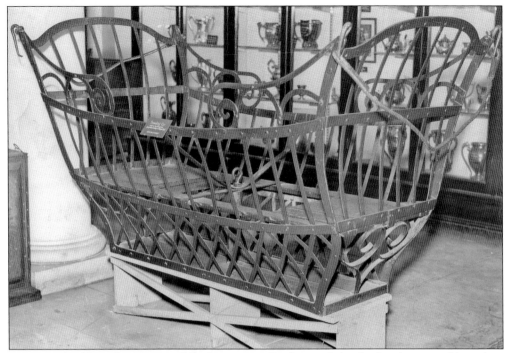

Engineers building the Niagara Falls Suspension Bridge used this basket (or moveable car) to carry workmen and their tools back and forth across the river on the first cables that spanned the gorge. When the basket was not in use for work purposes, men, women, and children were allowed to ride the basket back and forth for amusement.

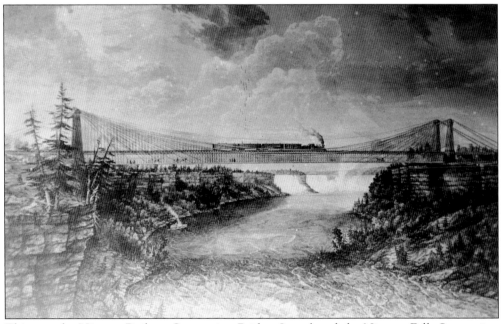

This was the Niagara Railway Suspension Bridge. It replaced the Niagara Falls Suspension Bridge in 1855. The lower deck was for carriages and pedestrians, while the upper deck was only for trains.

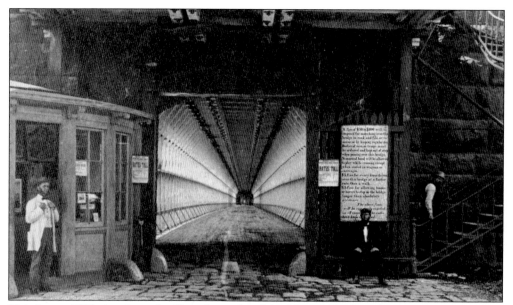

This is a c. 1855 view from the Canadian side of the Niagara Railway Suspension Bridge. The man in the white coat is standing in the entrance of the tollbooth. Leaning against the wall on the left are a broom and shovel used remove horse manure from the bridge deck. The list of bridge rules is above the seated man, including fines for marching in step or marching to music and fines for speeding on a horse at a rate faster than a walk.

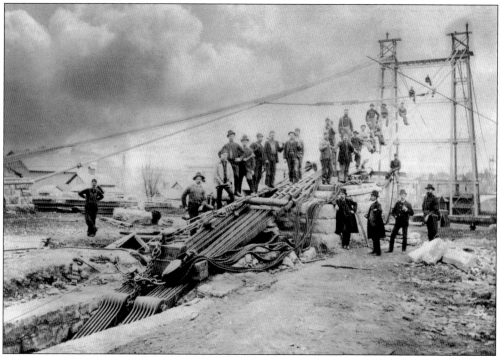

The Upper Suspension Bridge is under construction in 1868. Located about 900 feet below the American Falls, it opened on January 4, 1869. At 1,260 feet, it was the longest suspension bridge in the world. Its deck was only 10 feet wide, enough for one person walking along the side of a wagon.

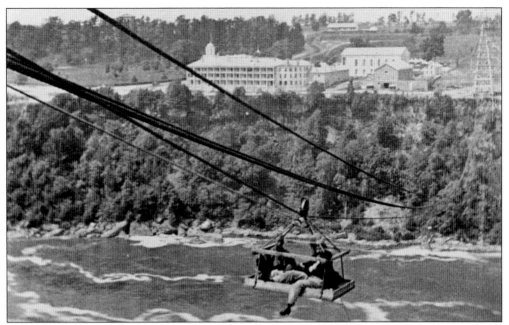

Pictured here in August 1869, a bridge official and the Chinese ambassador ride in a platform used by painters working on the cables for the Upper Suspension Bridge. In the background, on the Canadian side of the gorge, is the Clifton Hotel.

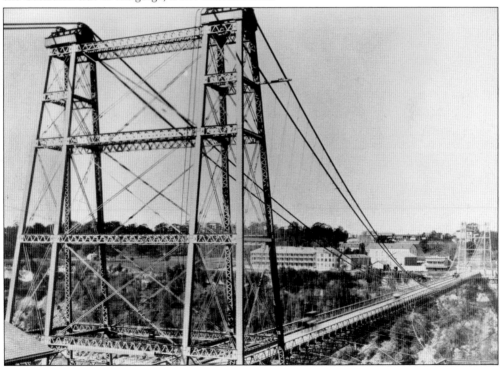

The Upper Suspension Bridge is shown here after its completion. The original towers were made of wood. In 1885, when the bridge was rebuilt, the towers were made of steel and enclosed with 100-foot-high observation decks, reached using elevators.

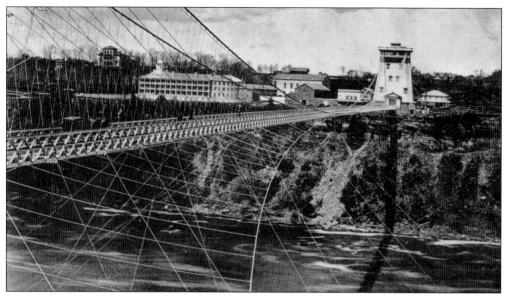

One of the enclosed towers of the Upper Suspension Bridge is pictured here c. 1885. A terrible windstorm on January 9, 1899, destroyed the Upper Suspension Bridge. The broken deck lay in the gorge on both sides. The bridge was rebuilt in just four months; it was replaced by the Upper Steel Arch Bridge in 1899.

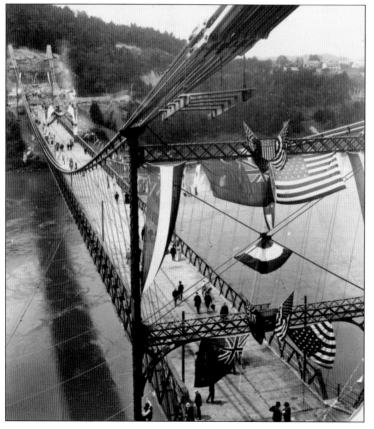

The Lewiston-Queenston Suspension Bridge was built in 1850, making it the second bridge to cross the Niagara Gorge. It was destroyed by a storm on April 16, 1864. Its few remains lingered until it was replaced in 1899 by the second Lewiston-Queenston Suspension Bridge. This photograph shows the opening day for the second bridge on July 21, 1899.

This 1883 photograph shows the Michigan Central Railway Cantilever Bridge, which was built about 200 feet south of the railway suspension bridge. It was the first cantilever bridge erected in the United States. After the Michigan Central Railway Arch Bridge opened in 1925, the cantilever bridge was torn down and sold for scrap.

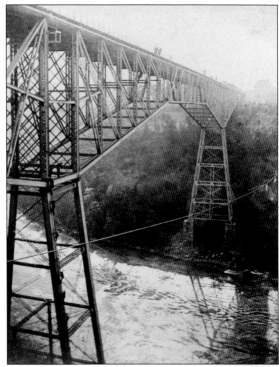

The Michigan Central Railway Arch Bridge was built in 1925. It was also known as the Canadian Pacific Railway Bridge, Con Rail Bridge, and Penn Central Railway Bridge.

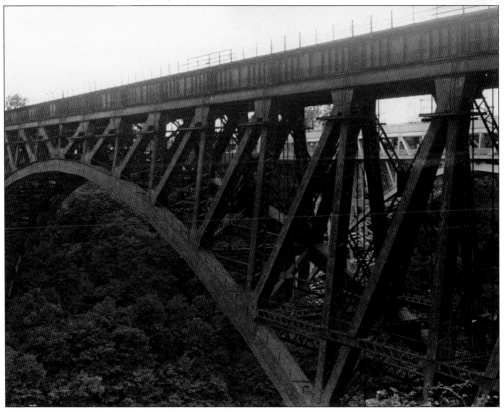

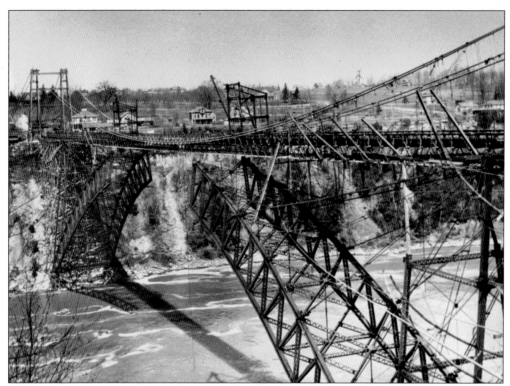

The Upper Steel Arch Bridge is under construction in 1888. It is also known as the Falls View Bridge and Honeymoon Bridge. When completed a year later, it was the longest single span arch in the world at 840 feet. It officially opened on July 1, 1899. The Upper Suspension Bridge was kept open until three weeks before the completion of the new bridge.

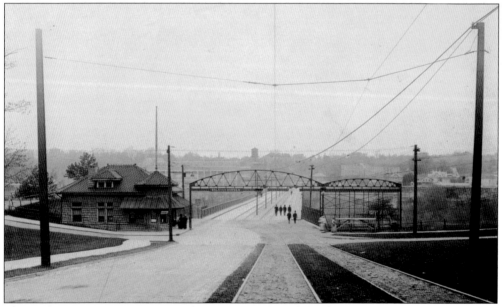

This is the American entrance to the Upper Steel Arch Bridge in 1900. The sign above the entrance demands that visitors walk their horse on this bridge.

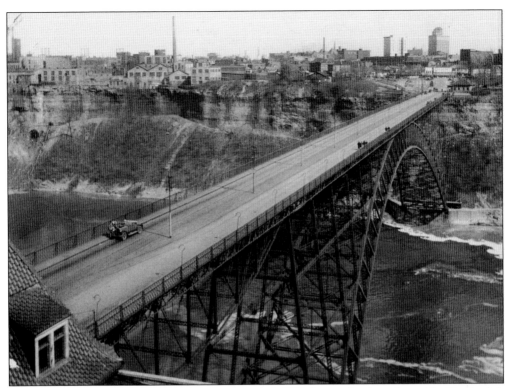

The Upper Steel Arch Bridge is shown here around 1920, facing the American side. On the left is the mill district; to the right is the shopping and tourist district. According to an article in the *Niagara Falls Gazette* from June 1, 1929, the bridge was deemed safe amongst rumors that were circulating about the magnitude of the bridge's sway. "The Falls View Bridge is, and will be kept, absolutely safe!" proclaimed the report from bridge engineers. This proclamation would be proved wrong less than 10 years later.

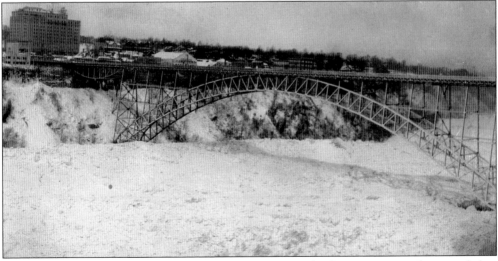

The Upper Steel Arch Bridge is shown in January 1938. The frozen waters in the gorge below were weakening the bridge supports when this photograph was taken. The bridge was doomed. Efforts to save it were futile. Local residents and newspaper reports waited for the inevitable.

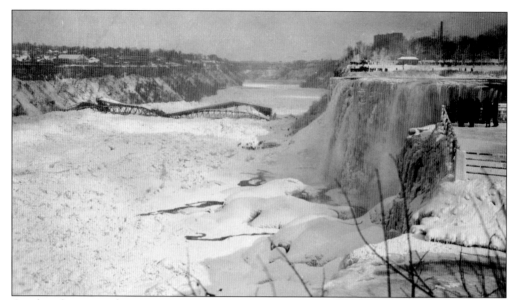

On the afternoon of January 27, 1938, the Upper Steel Arch Bridge slipped off its supports and fell below onto the massive ice bridge. This was the first time an ice bridge had destroyed a man-made bridge. While it was still possible to walk on the ice, wood and steel were salvaged. The wood was used to make souvenirs; the steel was sold for scrap. The rest of the bridge sank to the bottom of the river in the spring.

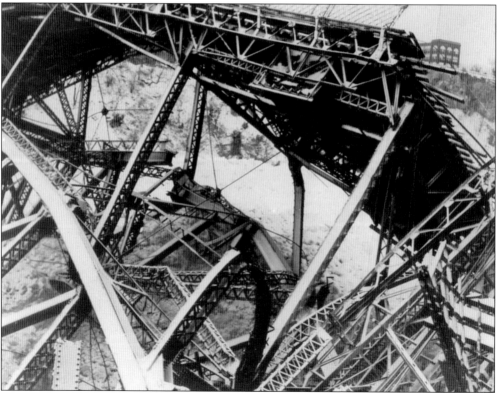

Here is a close-up of the Honeymoon Bridge, broken and lying on the ice in January 1938.

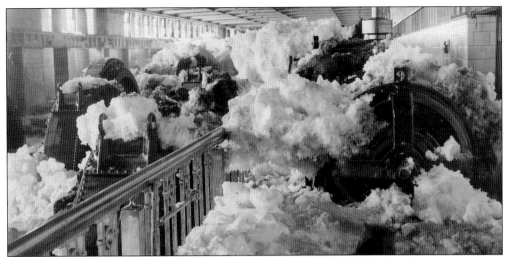

This photograph shows ice still inside the Ontario Power Company plant in the late spring of 1938, months after the ice bridge that had formed in January had forced its way through all the windows. Over $1 million in damage was done to the 15 generators. Today, the plant that sits below the Horseshoe Falls is no longer producing electricity.

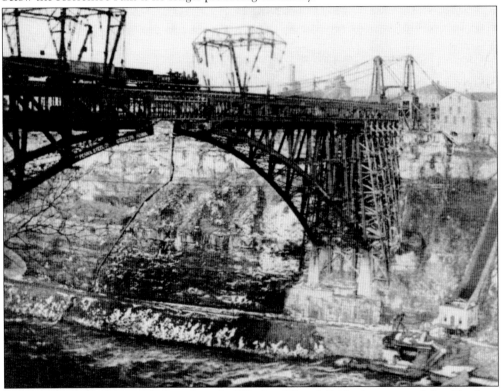

Taken in 1897, this photograph shows how the Whirlpool Rapids Bridge incorporated the old railway suspension bridge into its superstructure. Until 1937, the Whirlpool Rapids Bridge was known as the Niagara Railway Arch Bridge. The two boxlike structures on the bridge are called traveling cranes. Except for two hours every day, when railway workers replaced a piece of the track on the deck, there was no interruption in the flow of traffic during the construction of the bridge.

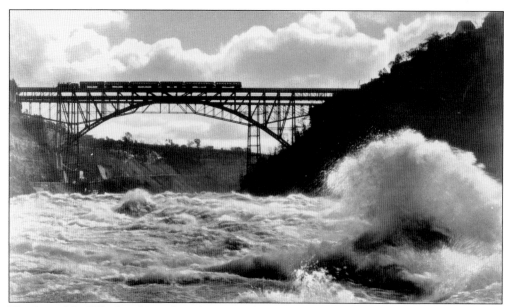

The fury of the Whirlpool Rapids is obvious in this photograph from the early 20th century. The cantilever bridge can be seen behind the Whirlpool Rapids Bridge. During Prohibition, trainloads of bottled alcoholic beverages were thrown into the rapids by American federal agents. As a result, there are thousands of broken bottles on the river bottom.

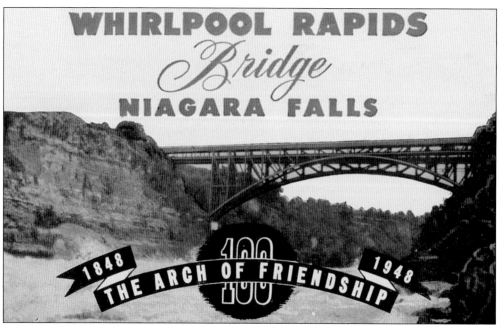

On August 2, 1948, the United States and Canada celebrated the 100th anniversary of this quick, all-weather route back and forth above the Niagara Gorge. This was the fourth bridge built on this site.

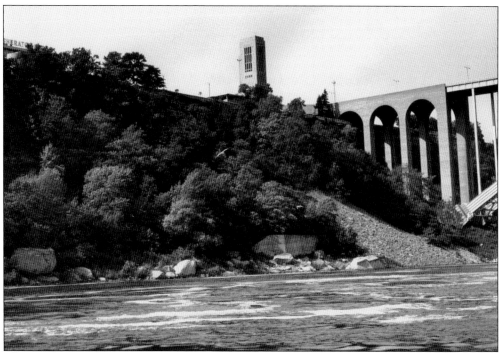

The Rainbow Bridge opened November 1, 1941. It is 550 feet north of the site of the Honeymoon Bridge. The concrete support from the Honeymoon Bridge is in the center of this 1950 photograph with the Rainbow Tower Carillon above. Also, note the bells of different sizes played by a carillonneur.

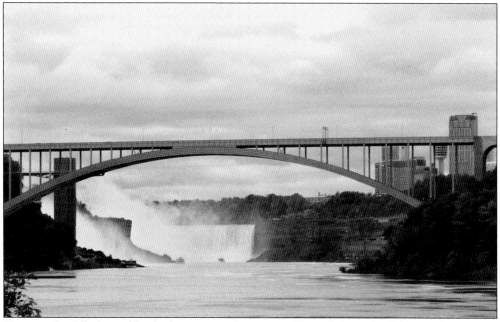

Here are the falls framed by the lower river, the gorge walls, and the arch of the Rainbow Bridge around 1950. The river just below the falls is over 100 feet deep. The depth is much less wherever there are rapids.

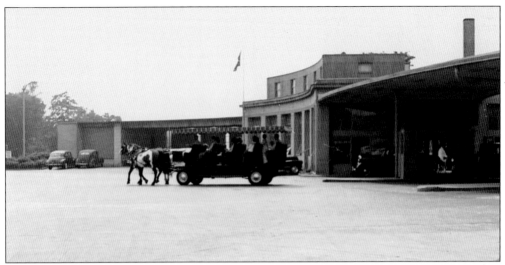

A horse-drawn touring vehicle enters the Rainbow Bridge from the Canadian side around 1948.

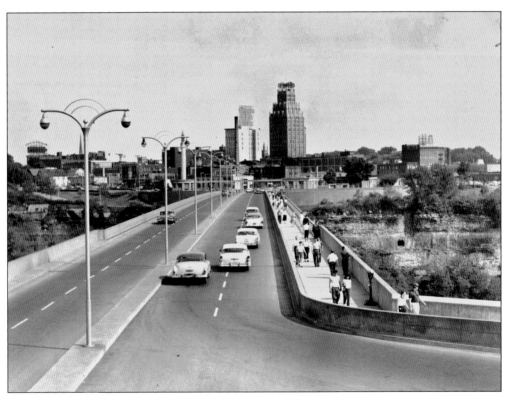

Pictured here is the entrance to the United States via the Rainbow Bridge around 1960. The tallest building in the background is the United Office Building, known today as the Giacomo, featuring a boutique-style hotel, apartments, and office space. The Walker Laundry smoke stack, the O'Keefe Ale Beer sign atop the Hancock Building, Falls Garage, and many other bustling businesses of the late 1950s are also visible in the background.

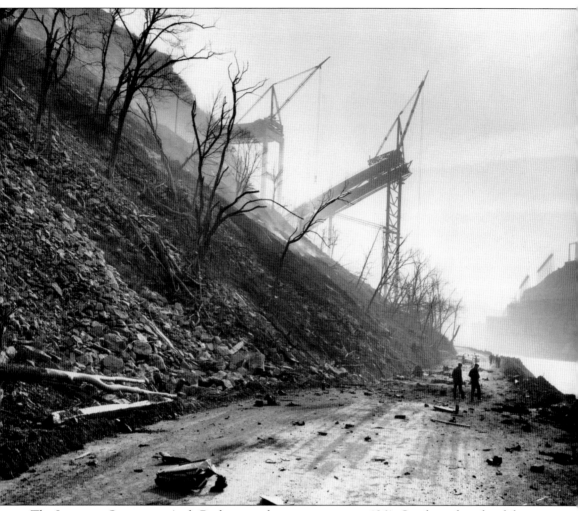

The Lewiston-Queenston Arch Bridge is under construction in 1961. On the right side of the photograph are the Sir Adam Beck I and Sir Adam Beck II hydroelectric power stations on the Canadian side of the gorge.

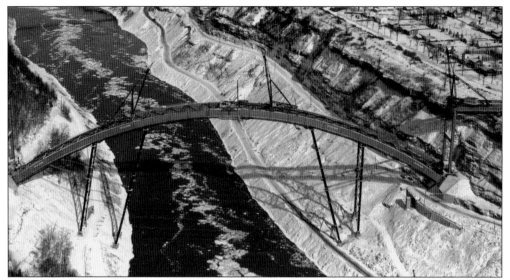

The Lewiston-Queenston Arch Bridge is pictured with the arch complete in 1962. Note how much deeper the gorge is here than by the falls.

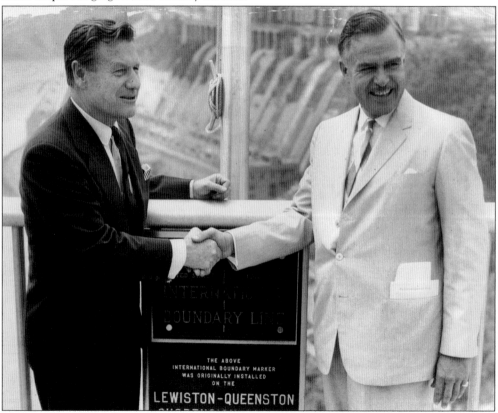

The Lewiston-Queenston Arch Bridge was completed and opened to traffic on November 1, 1962. The formal dedication of the bridge took place at the Canadian end on June 28, 1963. Here, New York governor Nelson Rockefeller (left) and Ontario premier John Robarts take time out to shake hands on the International Boundary Line.

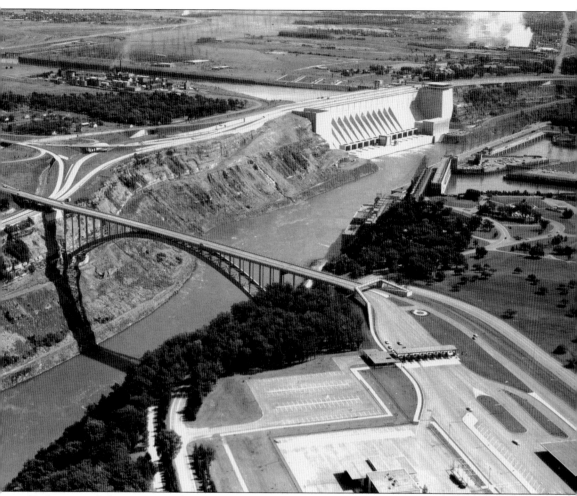

Highways and electric towers dominate the landscape in this early-1960s photograph. The Robert Moses Power Plant is to the left of the Sir Adam Beck I and Sir Adam Beck II power plants, split by the Niagara Gorge. The Lewiston-Queenston Arch Bridge spans the gorge through the center left of this photograph.

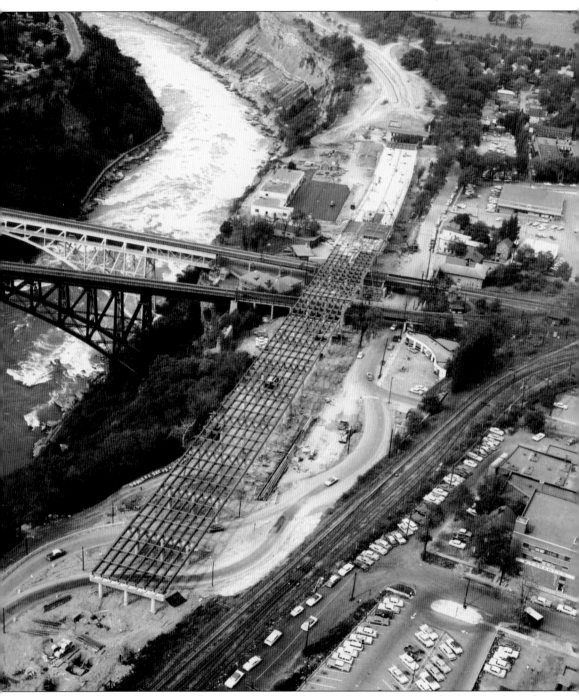

This c. 1960s photograph shows the Robert Moses Parkway overpass, which runs along the Niagara Gorge rim, under construction. On the left from top to bottom are the Whirlpool Rapids, Whirlpool Rapids Bridge, and Michigan Railway Bridge. The need and purpose of this parkway is one of the most debated topics still to this day, with residents calling for its removal. Almost 60 years after it was built, the man for which this roadway was named, Robert Moses, still remains one of the most polarizing figures in the history of the city of Niagara Falls.

Five

WINTER WONDERLAND

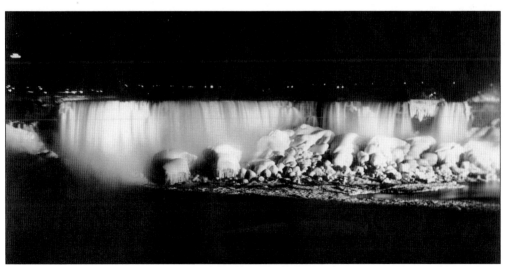

This photograph of the American Falls, illuminated at night, was taken in March 1931, about three months after a section of rock about 280 feet long dropped from the center of the falls, forming an indentation of about 70 feet into the crest line. Witnesses said a thunder-like rumble resulted, which was heard down the entire gorge all the way to Lake Ontario.

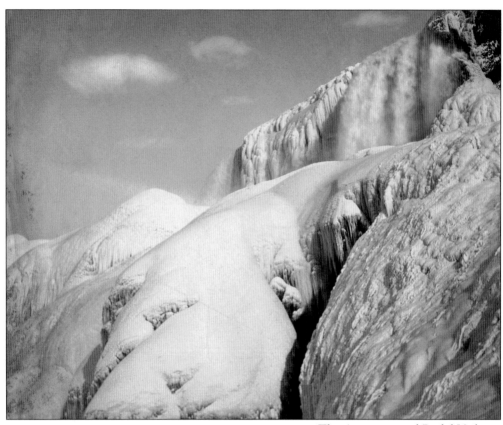

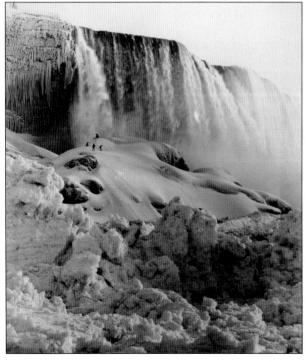

The American and Bridal Veil Falls are seen from the Cave of the Winds around 1900. Before ice in the river above the falls and rapids began to be controlled in the 1950s, the American and Bridal Veil Falls would sometimes freeze. Also, mounds of ice would form almost to the brink of the falls, not completely melting until late in the spring.

In this photograph from the early 20th century, a group of children play precariously close to the American Falls at the top of an ice mountain. Scenes like this were common when it was not against the law to play on these frozen playgrounds of ice and snow that formed around the falls.

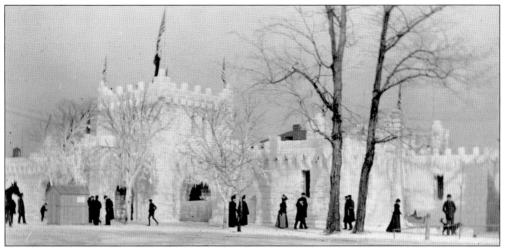

This beautiful ice palace was built in 1899 in the city of Niagara Falls, New York. It was 120 feet wide and 140 feet long. Its main tower was 55 feet high. An ice rink, 80 feet wide by 140 feet long, occupied most of the interior space. The rest was rented by vendors. The interior was adorned with colored ice and flowers frozen in cakes of ice. More than 2,000 electric lights illuminated the elaborate displays. Nearly 60 windows provided light for the palace during the day. Outside, the building was illuminated by one of the largest searchlights in the world. Admission to the palace was 60¢. It lasted until a "heat wave" in February.

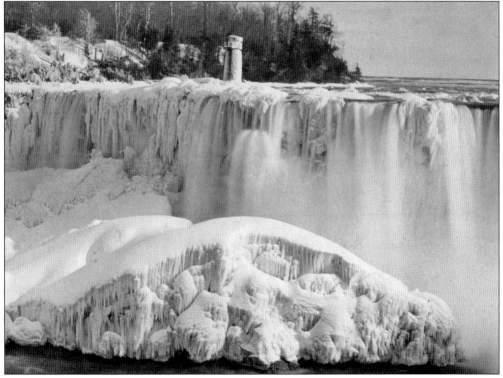

The stone tower is seen from the Canadian side around 1865. It was a popular place to view the Horseshoe Falls during all seasons, competing with Table Rock on the Canadian side. It was too dangerous to go into this tower in the winter.

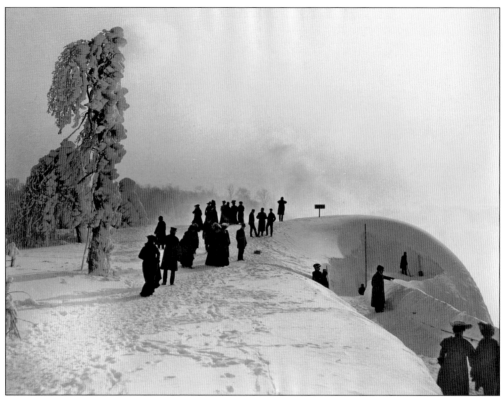

Prospect Point is pictured in winter early in the 20th century. The sign warns, "Danger." Niagara Falls draws tourists from all over the world in all seasons.

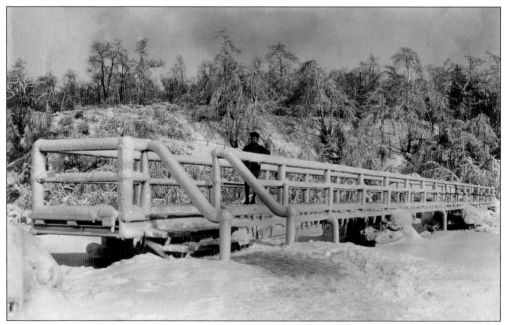

The bridge over Terrapin Rocks (now Terrapin Point) is shown around 1905. This part of the Horseshoe Falls was covered with fill in the 1950s.

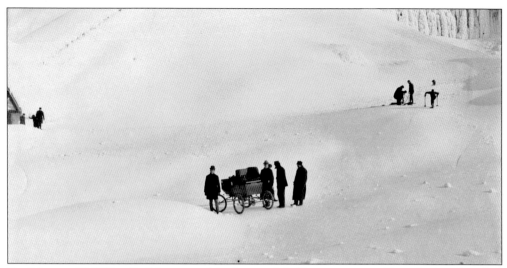

On February 27, 1901, a Buffalo agent of the Locomobile Company wanted his vehicle to be taken to the very top of the ice mountain below the American Falls. Although they only made it half way up, the "Locomobile" was proudly shown for onlookers and photographers—a great marketing idea that clearly came with an element of danger. To get to the mountain, the Locomobile was driven across the Upper Steel Arch Bridge to Canada, then down the inclined road to the *Maid of the Mist* dock. Then, with great care, it was driven across the ice bridge to the mountain. To get up the mountain, six men used ropes and tackles. Children and families play in the distance on the frigid snow, some using skis or snowshoes.

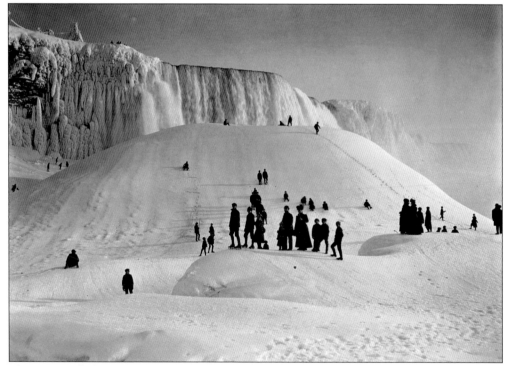

The ice mound below Prospect Point was clearly a popular place for winter fun in the late 1800s. Thousands of thrill seekers would come by train on the weekends throughout the winter months.

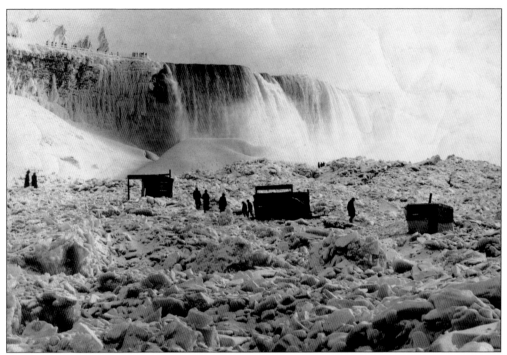

According to the *Niagara Falls Gazette* of February 14, 1883, "A sharp rogue is that who has built a shanty of boards right in the center of the massive ice bridge at the Falls, and freely sells liquor to all who apply for it without the formality of a license. He is right on the line between two countries, and thus evades the law of both."

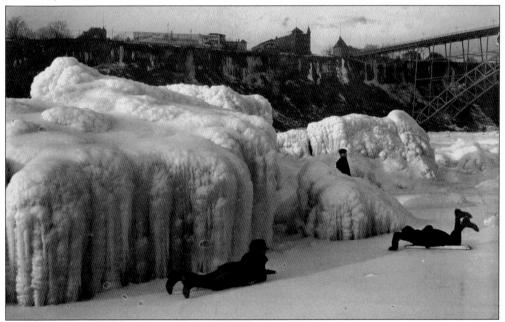

Boys ride their sleds on the ice bridge in the late 1800s. The ice bridges are made from ice floes from Lake Erie that freeze together after going over the falls. Some of them went as far north as Lake Ontario.

On February 4, 1912, people were walking on the ice bridge when it suddenly broke into pieces, one of which began to move downriver with four people on it: Eldridge and Clara Stanton of Toronto, Burrell Heacock of Cleveland, and Ignatius Roth, Heacock's friend. Roth was saved by local river man Red Hill Sr. The other three perished.

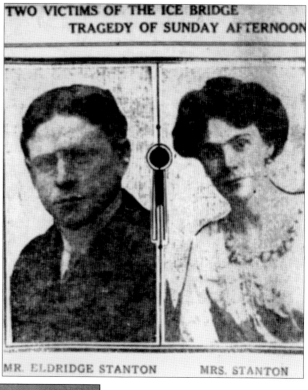

TWO VICTIMS OF THE ICE BRIDGE TRAGEDY OF SUNDAY AFTERNOON

MR. ELDRIDGE STANTON   MRS. STANTON

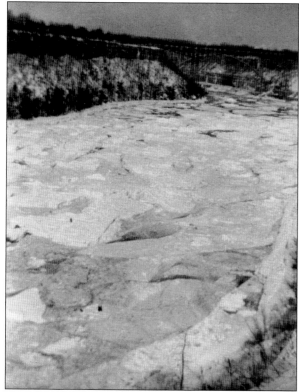

The Stantons can be seen holding onto each other on the lower left floe; Burrel Heacock can be seen just farther up to the left. Since this accident, it has been against the law to go on an ice bridge.

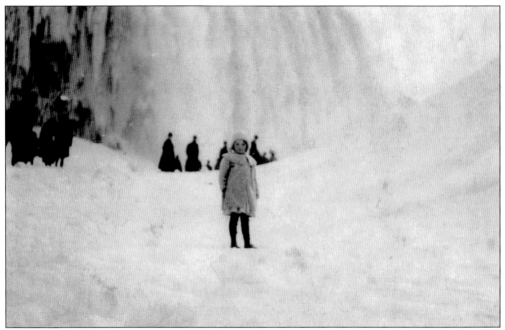

Christine Coulter Stevens, age seven, stands for a photograph taken on February 4, 1912, just hours before the tragic accident on the ice bridge. Christine and her family just arrived back at their nearby home after visiting the falls when they heard the news about the tragedy.

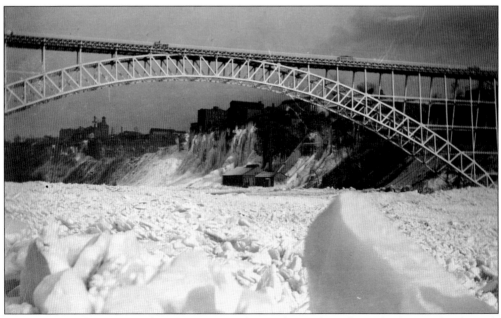

The Falls View (Honeymoon) Bridge is pictured around 1900 from the ice bridge. Under the arch of the bridge, the mill district can be seen in the background.

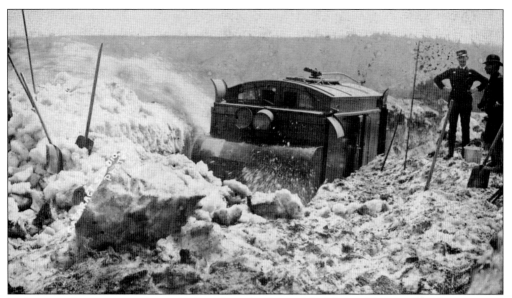

This rotary plow was removing an ice jam along the shore of the Niagara River in 1899. Ice jams used to destroy boat docks along the shores of the Niagara River, both above and below the falls.

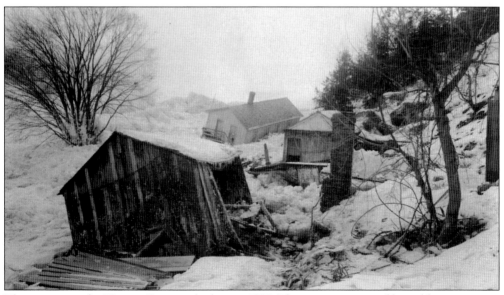

This ice jam in the Niagara River took place in 1883. The jams were caused by sudden movement of ice from Lake Erie into the river, usually pushed by strong southwest winds.

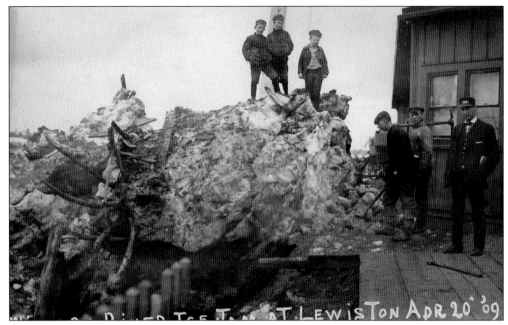

An ice jam like this one was a common sight in the early 20th century. The "Ice Boom" at the source of the river now prevents jamming and shoreline damage. The Ice Boom is a series of floating barrels used to control the movement of the ice from Lake Erie.

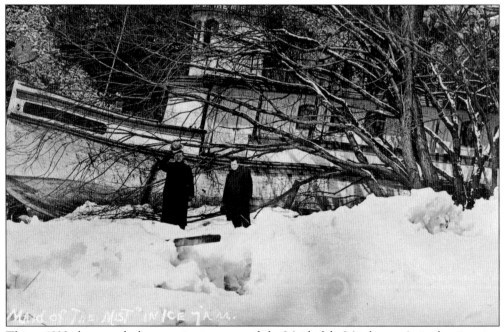

This c. 1890 photograph shows an ice jam around the *Maid of the Mist* boats. A similar situation in January 1938 resulted in the collapse of the Falls View (Honeymoon) Bridge.

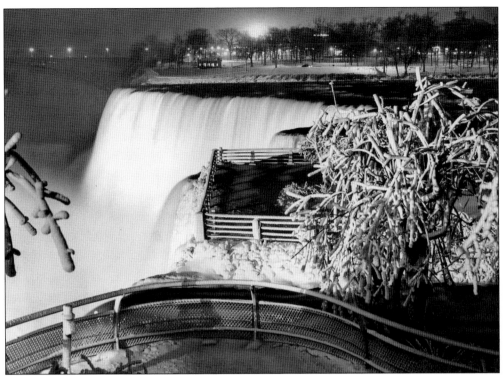

Here is a winter view of the American Falls from Goat Island in 1954. When the mist freezes on trees, it forms an ice called rime. The weight of the ice makes the trees bow to the river.

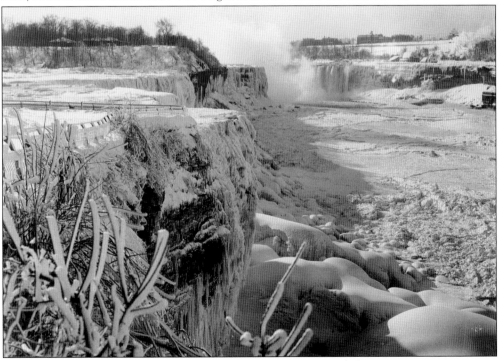

The American Falls is almost completely frozen in this photograph from 1930.

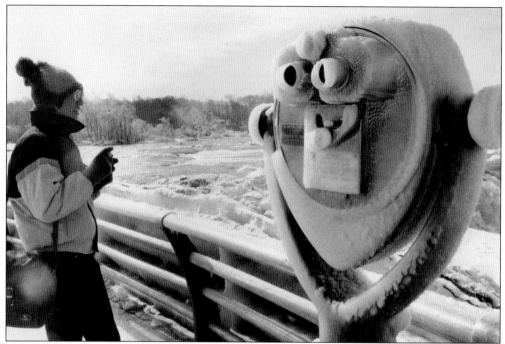

This Japanese tourist visited the falls on a frozen winter day, March 2, 1985. He is standing at Prospect Point next to a frozen, coin-operated viewer. Many of these viewers can be seen along the railings in the state park, giving visitors close-up perspectives of the beauty of Niagara Falls.

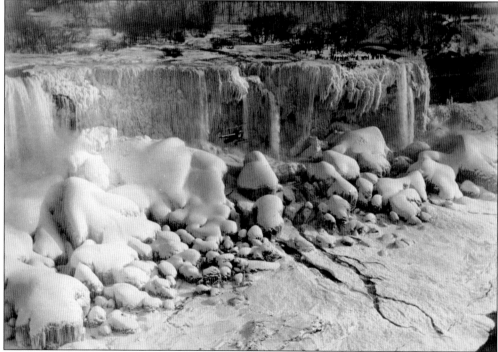

In this 1947 photograph, a helicopter flying close to the falls (center) gets a close-up view of the low-running, almost totally frozen waters of the American Falls.

Six

PEOPLE AND PLACES

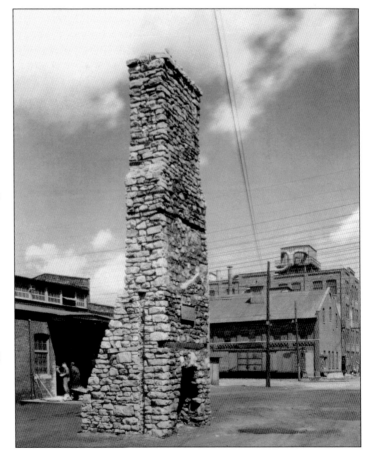

The Old Stone Chimney is surrounded by the industrial buildings of the Carborundum Company in 1940. It was originally attached to a French barracks at Fort Little Niagara. That fort was burned in the French and Indian War in 1759. Only the chimney survived. The chimney has been moved twice since. It now stands along an overgrown highway embankment of the Robert Moses Parkway. Currently, plans are underway to move it to a more deserving location.

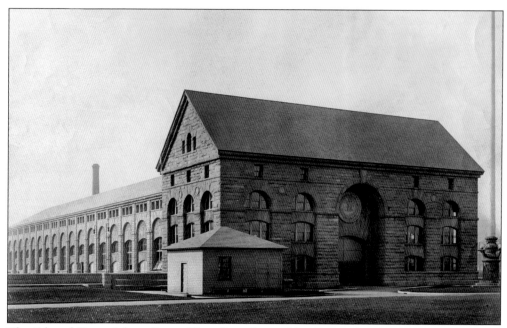

The Edward Dean Adams Power Plant Powerhouse No. 1, completed in 1895, was the first alternating current hydroelectric plant in the world. It was on the shore of the Niagara River, about 1.5 miles above the American Falls. The alternating current was produced using a process invented by Nikola Tesla. The electricity from this plant was used in 1901 to light up the Pan American Exposition in Buffalo.

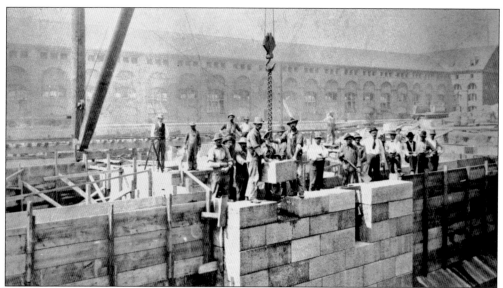

Men work on the construction of the Edward Dean Adams Power Plant Powerhouse No. 2. It was completed in 1904. Stanford White, the most prominent architect in the world in late 1800s, designed the power plant.

This statue of Nikola Tesla was a gift to the United States from the people of Yugoslavia in commemoration of the bicentennial in July 1976. Tesla made it possible to transmit electricity long distances. Tesla also worked with George Westinghouse on the development of the Edward Dean Adams power plants. The main entrance or portal from the Edward Dean Adams Power Plant Powerhouse No. 1 was moved to Goat Island in 1967. Here, it can be seen behind Tesla's statue.

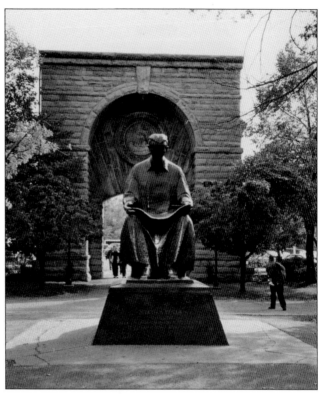

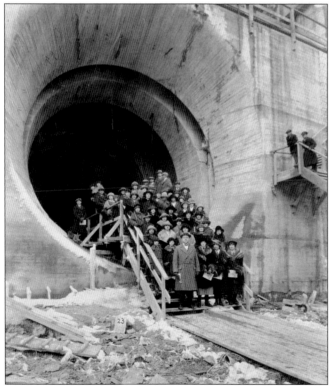

Mr. and Mrs. Kelley and the students of the Kelley Business Institute are pictured in 1923. They are standing in the entrance of the new power tunnel built to send water to the Schoellkopf Power Plant. This tunnel made it unnecessary to widen the canal from the upper Niagara River to the recently enlarged power plant.

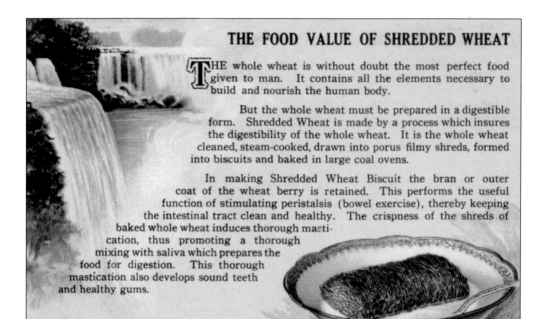

THE FOOD VALUE OF SHREDDED WHEAT

THE whole wheat is without doubt the most perfect food given to man. It contains all the elements necessary to build and nourish the human body.

But the whole wheat must be prepared in a digestible form. Shredded Wheat is made by a process which insures the digestibility of the whole wheat. It is the whole wheat cleaned, steam-cooked, drawn into porus filmy shreds, formed into biscuits and baked in large coal ovens.

In making Shredded Wheat Biscuit the bran or outer coat of the wheat berry is retained. This performs the useful function of stimulating peristalsis (bowel exercise), thereby keeping the intestinal tract clean and healthy. The crispness of the shreds of baked whole wheat induces thorough mastication, thus promoting a thorough mixing with saliva which prepares the food for digestion. This thorough mastication also develops sound teeth and healthy gums.

The production of Shredded Wheat began in Niagara Falls, New York, in 1901 at the Natural Food Company, founded by Henry D. Perky. It later became the Shredded Wheat Company. The original factory was a beautiful, yellow-brick building with a multitude of windows. This company set new standards for excellent workplace conditions and employee appreciation.

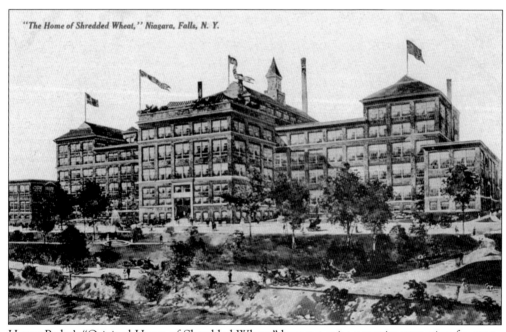

"The Home of Shredded Wheat," Niagara, Falls, N. Y.

Henry Perky's "Original Home of Shredded Wheat" became quite a tourist attraction for many years. The main entrance resembled that of a fancy hotel.

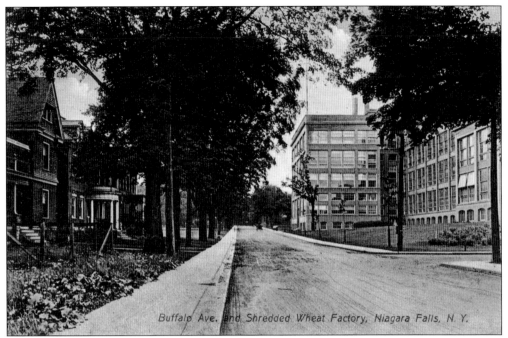

Buffalo Ave. and Shredded Wheat Factory, Niagara Falls, N. Y.

The original Shredded Wheat factory was located on Buffalo Avenue in the early 1900s. This building was closed in 1954. Production from then on took place in the new buildings in both Niagara Falls, New York, and Niagara Falls, Canada.

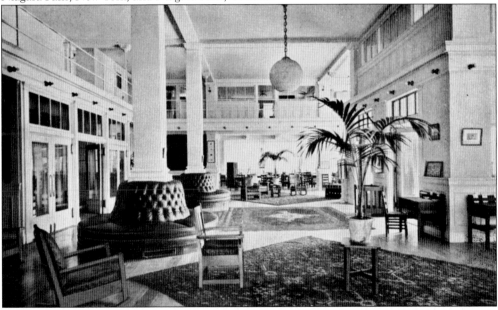

This is the foyer and reception room of the Shredded Wheat factory on Buffalo Avenue. It resembled a five-star hotel. Guided tours were provided for visitors, which included a free lunch and a walk through the 1,000-seat auditorium, rooftop patio, and garden. Writing and reading rooms for guests, furnished with beautiful rugs and sumptuous, weathered-oak, leather-upholstered furniture were on either side of the reception room. From the middle of the ceiling hung a pendant, a great crystal ball, inside of which were 36 electric lights.

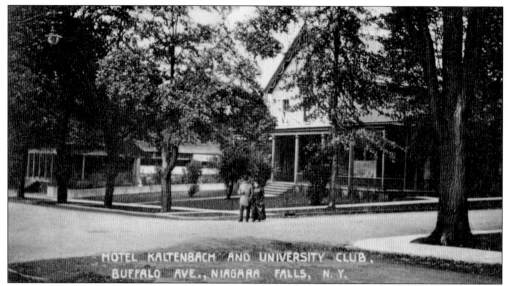

Andrew Kaltenback opened the Hotel Kaltenback in 1878. He boasted that his place had "many of the best features of German hostelries." A roomy veranda overlooked the American Rapids and a large lawn known as the "Kaltenback Green," the site of many concerts by the famous Shredded Wheat Band. The Kaltenback was torn down in the early 1920s to make room for the construction of the Red Coach Inn.

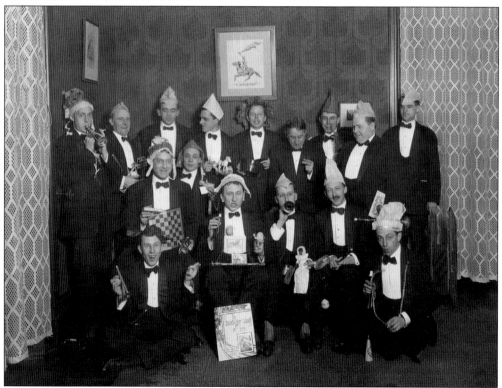

The University Club celebrates the arrival of a new year in 1910. The University Club, a group of university graduates, gathered in the Hotel Kaltenback for many years in the early 1900s.

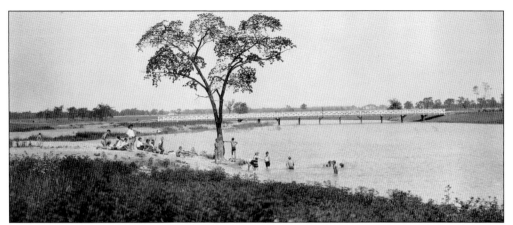

Children swim in Hyde Park Lake in 1931. The park had been formally dedicated on September 7, 1929, located on land left to the city in the will of Charles B. Hyde. The park has grown through the years and now includes a stadium, golf courses, picnic grounds with shelters, a swimming pool, a senior citizens center, tennis courts, indoor ice hockey rinks, bocce courts, and volleyball courts.

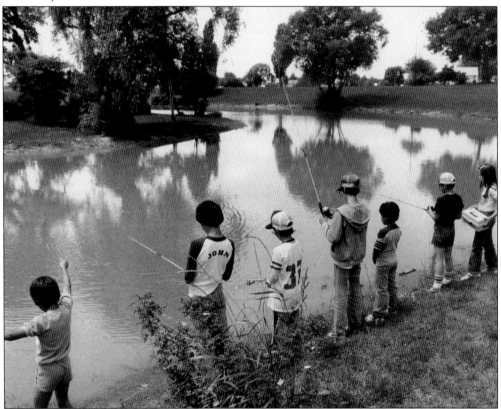

From 1980 to 1983, the City of Niagara Falls cleaned up the lake in Hyde Park. In this 1982 photograph, children fish along the bank of the lake. Hyde Park Lake was made in the 1920s by constructing a dam in Gill Creek, which empties into the Niagara River above the falls. The southeast end of Hyde Park along Pine Avenue was once a campground called Camp Jones. More than 41,000 tourists visited Camp Jones in its first year.

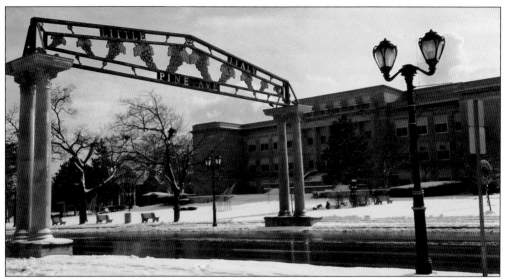

The stretch of Pine Avenue between Hyde Park Boulevard and Portage Road in the city of Niagara Falls, New York, is known as Little Italy. Early in the city's history, this is the area where Italian emigrants settled and raised their families. A portion of this street is closed every summer for a popular Italian festival. The building to the right is the former Niagara Falls High School, now known as the Niagara Arts and Cultural Center.

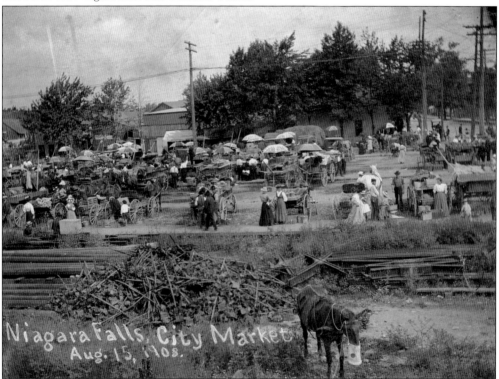

This is the Niagara Falls City Market on August 15, 1908. Farmers brought their produce and other foods in horse-drawn wagons long before "supermarkets" became the popular way to buy and sell fresh food.

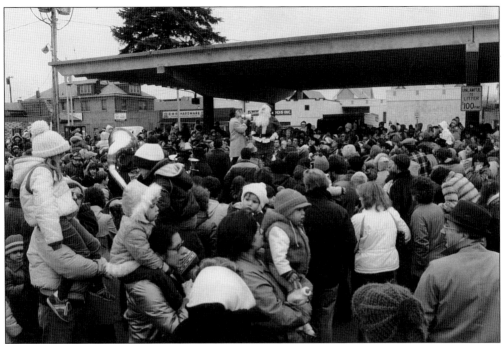

This huge crowd gathered at the Niagara Falls City Market in 1981 to greet Santa Claus.

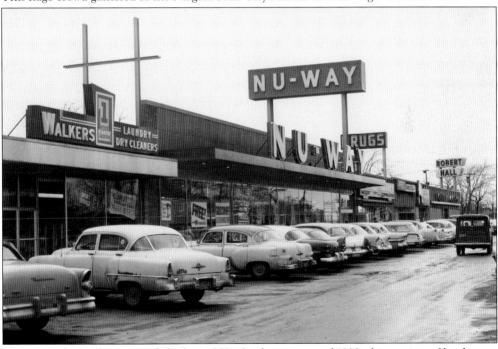

This is Haeberle Plaza around the late 1950s. In the summer of 1923, this section of land was a field where evangelists held a six-week campaign starting in mid-September. They built a 234-foot-long tabernacle on this site to accommodate upwards of 6,000 people who would come for the religious services. After the campaign ended, the contractor used the salvaged lumber of the tabernacle to build concrete forms for the construction of the Hotel Niagara.

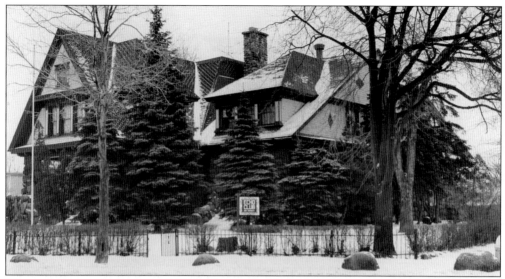

This mansion on the corner of Welch Avenue and Portage Road was built in 1893. It is made of glacial boulders and stones gathered from the surrounding lands. Its original owner, Thomas Vincent Welch, was a local businessman and politician. He was instrumental in obtaining enacting legislation for the establishment of the Niagara Reservation State Park in 1885 and was appointed the first superintendent of the Niagara State Reservation.

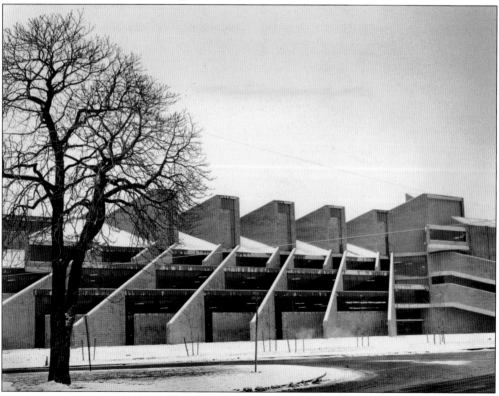

On March 9, 1974, the Earl W. Brydges building, designed by architect Paul Rudolph, officially became the home of the Niagara Falls Public Library.

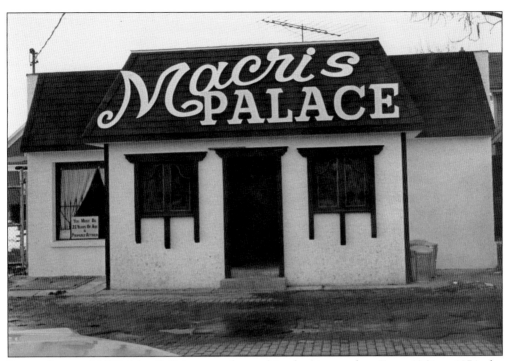

Pictured around 1975, Macri's Palace was located in the city market. From 1964 to 1974, the restaurant was known as DelFredo's on Main Street before moving to the city market and becoming Macri's Palace. From 2005 to 2009, it was located in the Summit Mall. Today, this popular restaurant is located on Center Street in historic Lewiston.

Max M. Oppenheim stands in front of his business at 1909 Main Street around 1924. In 1941, Oppenheim toured America and was attracted by the crowds that flocked to the city zoos. He thought about creating a privately owned zoo, open to the public, with free parking facilities. When he returned from his tour, he purchased 83 acres on Niagara Falls Boulevard, east of the Bell Aircraft Plant, accessible to persons in Niagara and Erie Counties for zoo and farm purposes.

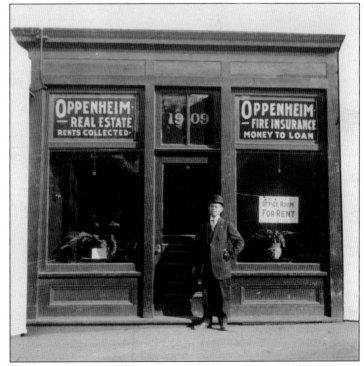

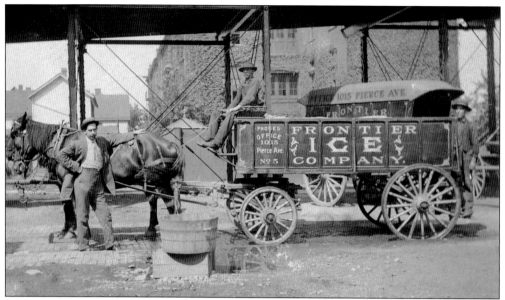

The Frontier Ice Company was located at 1015 Pierce Avenue in 1909. Ice was delivered by horse-drawn wagons to homes and businesses throughout Niagara Falls. Iceboxes kept food cold or frozen at that time.

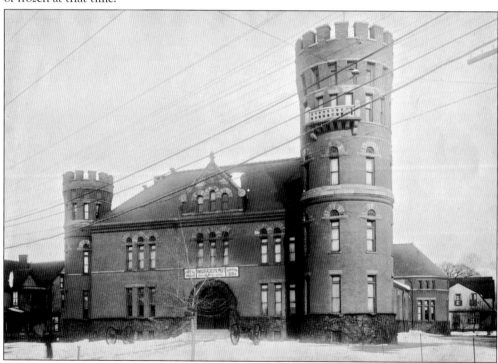

The first armory in Niagara Falls was built in 1887 on the corner of Walnut and Sixth Streets. It was replaced by the one in this 1895 photograph, taking over as the home of the 42nd Separate Company of the National Guard. The building was rented for numerous activities in the early 1900s. As noted in the sign above the front door, admission to the dance after the athletic meet was only 25¢.

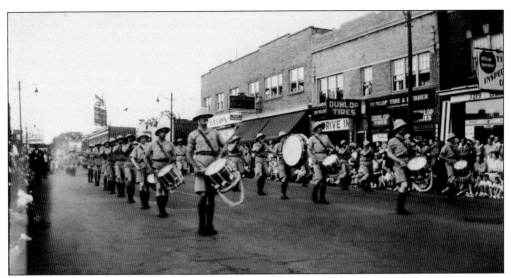

The Elks Parade goes down Main Street in 1943. In the background are, from left to right, Loblaw's grocer, Harris and Lever Florists (still existing today), and a Dunlop Tire & Rubber Corporation service store.

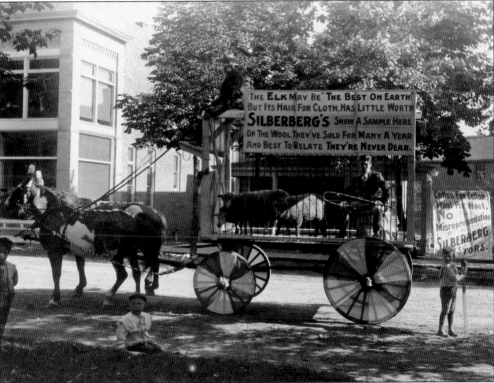

Silberberg's was by far the largest of the men's clothing stores in Niagara Falls from 1900 to 1958. It occupied an entire block of Main Street when in operation. The sign above the wagon proclaims, "The Elk may be the best on Earth, but its hair for cloth has little worth. Silberberg's show a sample here, of the wool they've sold for many a year, and best to relate they're never dear." The boy's sign says, "Cotton for cotton, wool for wool, no misrepresentation at the Silberberg store!"

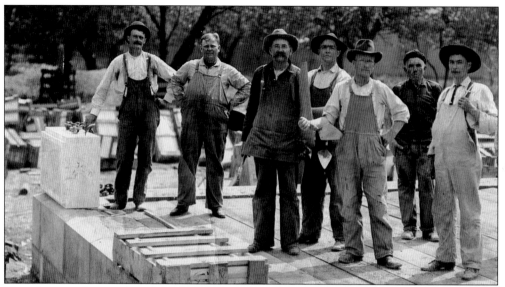

This photograph was taken the day the cornerstone was laid for the Federal Building in the city of Niagara Falls in 1906. It has served as the main post office ever since its completion. The first post office in Niagara Falls opened in 1808 in the house of Augustus Porter. At that time, the community of Niagara Falls was known as Manchester.

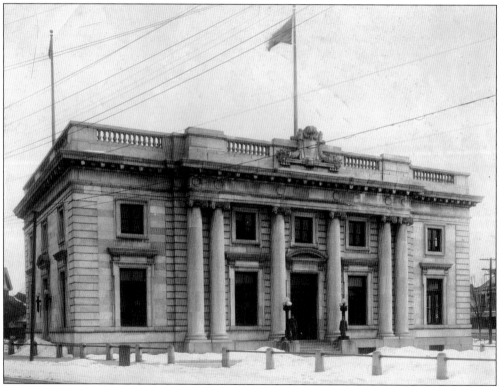

The completed Federal Building housed the US Post Office around 1910. This white marble building on Main Street is the best example of Beaux-Arts architecture in the city. The architect was James Knox Taylor.

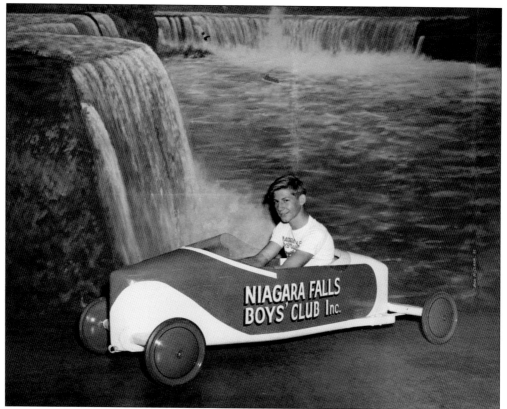

Here is the soapbox derby champ of 1946. For many years in the middle of the 20th century, the city sponsored the races that were very popular. The races were often held on Hyde Park Boulevard, starting at the bridge just above North Avenue. The entrants had to build the cars themselves.

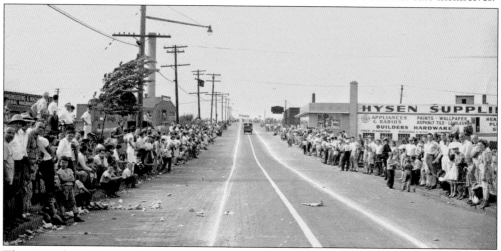

This 1949 photograph shows Hyde Park Boulevard to the north during a soapbox derby. Note the cobblestone bricks that made up the surface of the street. Hyde Park Boulevard was originally called Sugar Street because sugar leaked from bags on wagons going north to Fort Niagara. The street went from a dock by the Niagara River straight to the original portage road. The name was changed when Hyde Park opened in the 1920s.

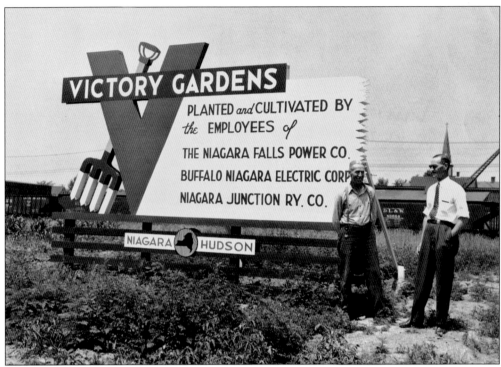

The victory gardens were vegetable and flower gardens planted during the World War I and World War II to help support the war effort. The one in this photograph was located on Buffalo Avenue during World War II. During this war, almost 20 million Americans planted victory gardens. Their efforts growing and preserving their own food helped to save products needed by the armed forces. The gardens came in all sizes and shapes, from window boxes to large community plots, such as the one seen here.

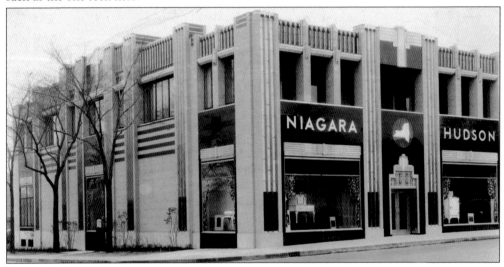

The Niagara Hudson Power Company was organized in 1929 by Paul Schoellkopf, head of the Niagara Falls Power Company. In 1930, the Niagara Hudson office was located in this building on the corner of Ferry Avenue and Third Street. Niagara Hudson became a part of Niagara Mohawk in 1950.

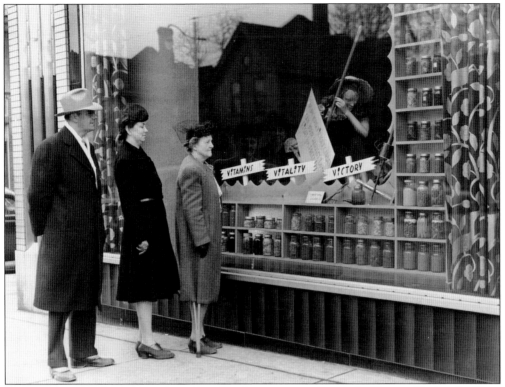

Shoppers take a look at the goods produced by the victory gardens at the Niagara Hudson Building on the corner of Ferry Avenue and Third Street in 1945. The sign in the window says, "Plan your victory garden, can your harvest to fight for freedom!" Note the reflection in the window of the houses on the opposite side of Third Street.

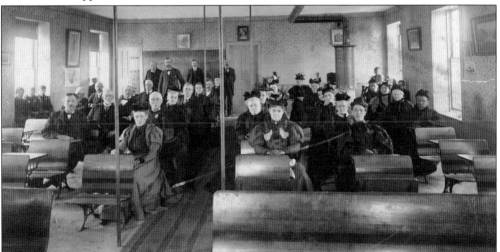

The seven-room Third Street School was located on the east side of the street between Falls Street and Jefferson Avenue (Rainbow Boulevard). Thomas Vincent Welch, one of the most active citizens in the history of the city of Niagara Falls, is seated at this meeting inside the school's main room around 1897, fourth from the front on the left side of the aisle. Seated in the first row on the left is Miss Oppenheim (sister of Max) and behind her is James F. Trott.

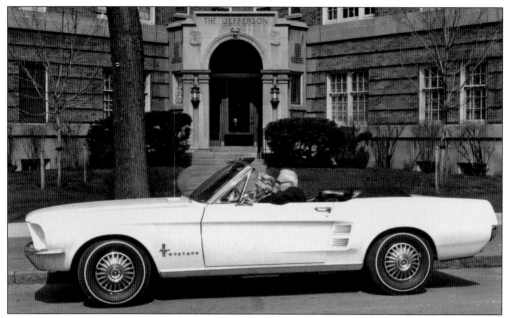

Mrs. Kinsey, pictured here at age 90, and Victor Albert sit in a brand new sports car, a 1967 Ford Mustang, parked in front of the Jefferson Apartments. Mrs. Kinsey's husband, Eugene, was an early automotive pioneer in the area who designed and built a car called "The Niagara" in his LaSalle factory at the start of the 20th century.

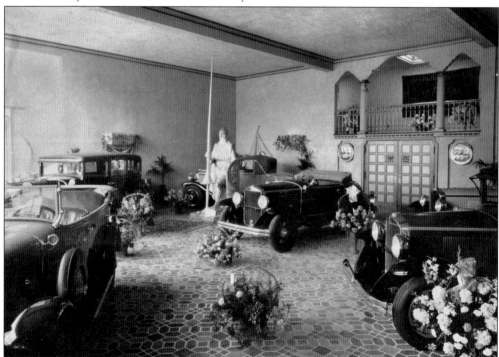

This is Kinsey's showroom on Main Street in 1903. Eugene Kinsey manufactured both passenger cars and racing models. Note how somber looking the room is, a far cry from how flashy and over the top automobile showrooms look today.

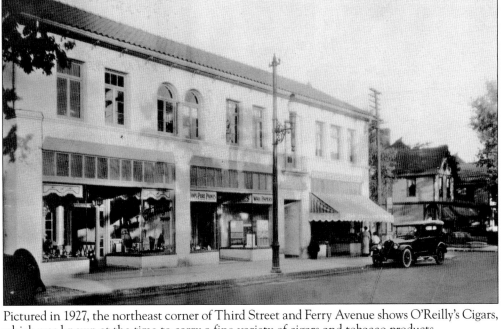

Pictured in 1927, the northeast corner of Third Street and Ferry Avenue shows O'Reilly's Cigars, which was known at the time to carry a fine variety of cigars and tobacco products.

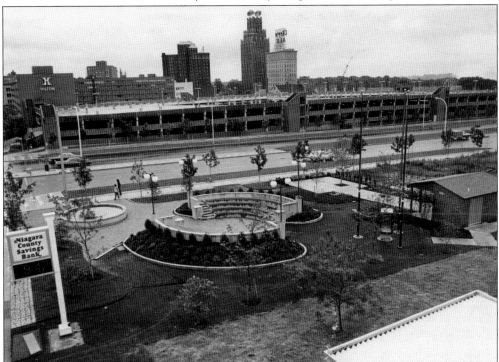

This 1976 photograph of the Savings Bank Park was taken from the corner of Third and Niagara Streets. The Hilton Hotel (now the Sheraton Hotel), the Parkway Apartments, the Hotel Niagara, and the United Office Building (now the Giacomo) are in the background. The large parking structure just opposite Niagara Street no longer exists.

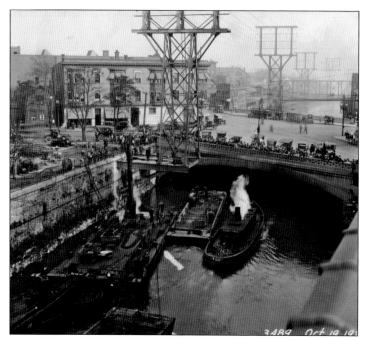

The Hydraulic Canal at the corner of Niagara and Third Streets is shown here on October 19, 1920. The towers carried electricity from the hydroelectric power plant at the bottom of the gorge to other cities. The canal was built in stages during the 19th century and brought water from above the falls to mills and power plants at the top and bottom of the gorge. The barges took supplies and goods to the powerhouses and businesses along the canal. (Courtesy of the *Niagara Gazette*.)

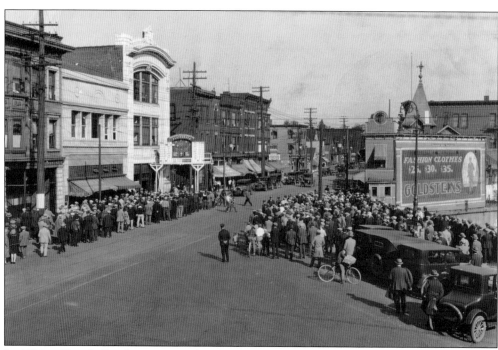

In 1920, a Play-O-Graph was erected in front of the *Gazette*'s building. Crowds often jammed Niagara Street as they listened to the megaphone service offering a play-by-play account of baseball games or punch-by-punch details of boxing matches. (Courtesy of the *Niagara Gazette*.)

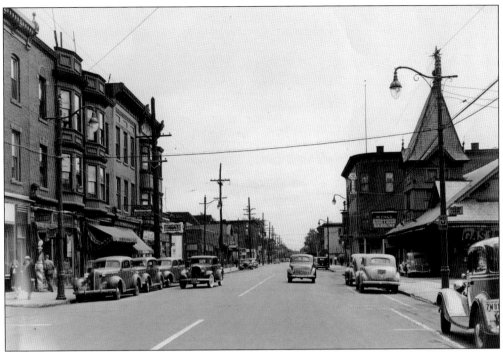

Looking east on Niagara Street from Third Street, the newly installed streetlights are shown around 1940. All the buildings on the right side of the photograph are now gone, replaced by the Seneca Niagara Casino today.

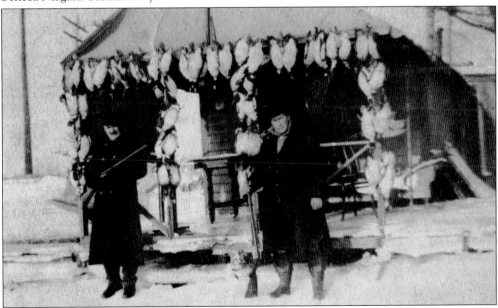

Gill Creek runs north to south, dividing the city in two. It meandered quite a bit before it was straightened and deepened. There was also an island where it emptied into the Niagara River. Both fishing and the hunting of ducks and geese were popular on the island and along the creek. The boathouse shown here was near the mouth of the creek in the late 19th century. This area was covered over with fill after the Robert Moses Parkway was built in the early 1960s.

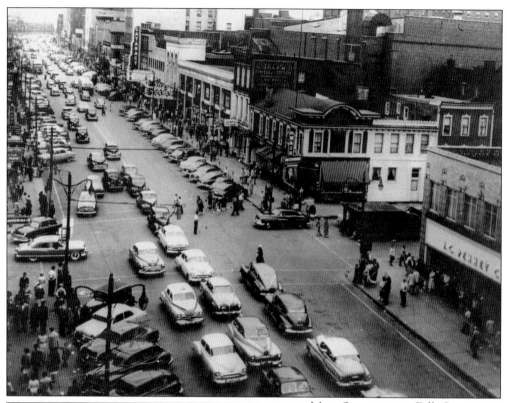

Main Street crosses Falls Street in the center of this 1954 photograph. Note at right the Main Restaurant, which was once popular with local young adults and tourists. Also, in the background amongst the many businesses, the Strand and Cataract Theaters are visible along the right side of the street. In between Main Restaurant and J.C. Penney's are underground public restrooms in the middle of Main Street. (Courtesy of the Jacob family.)

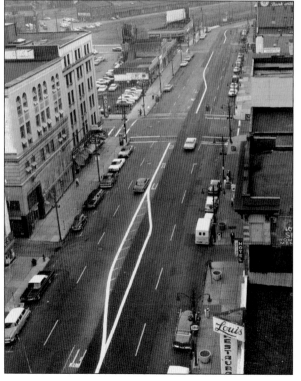

The tallest building on the left is the Imperial Hotel. To its left is the JN Adams Department Store. This stretch of Falls Street was once the busiest in the city of Niagara Falls. The buildings, seen here in 1965, were mostly all demolished in the ill-fated urban renewal project of the 1960s.

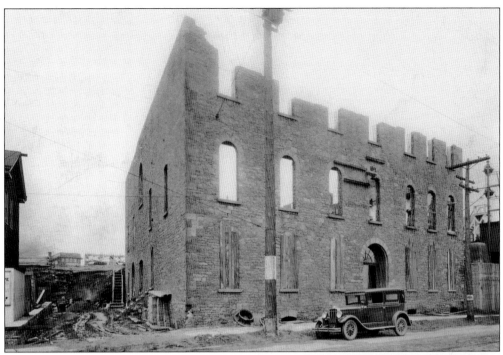

The Customs House is being repaired after a fire in December 1929. It was built in 1863 and served inspectors for the Niagara Falls Suspension Bridge, Niagara Cantilever Bridge, Whirlpool Rapids Bridge, and Michigan Central Railway Bridge at various points in its history. With Niagara Falls receiving the second highest amount of American imports at one point, the Customs House was once a very busy post for its inspectors. It is now the location of the Underground Railroad Interpretive Center.

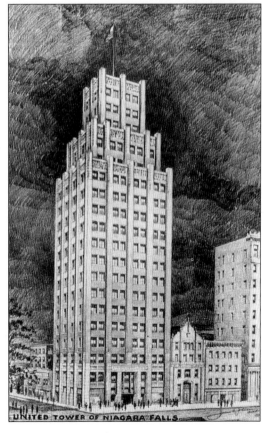

The United Office Building is pictured here around 1999. Designed by architect James A. Johnson, it was completed in 1929 on the eve of the Great Depression. The building is one of the most important landmarks in downtown Niagara Falls. It now contains upscale apartments, office space, and the Giacomo, a luxury boutique hotel. This building can be seen in almost every photograph of the city of Niagara Falls skyline since 1929.

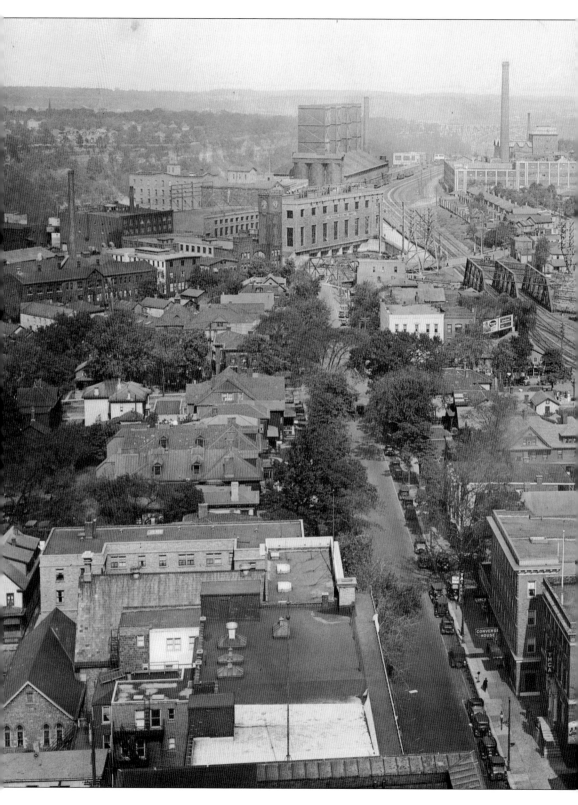

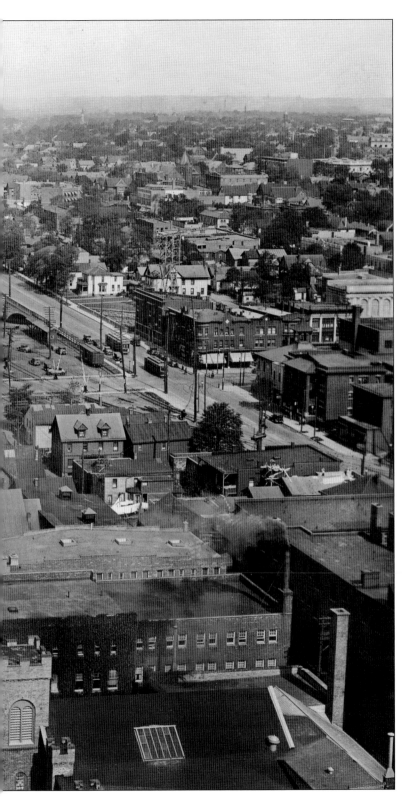

Taken from the United Office Building, the city of Niagara Falls is pictured here in the early 1930s. At the bottom right of the photograph is the First Presbyterian Church and above that are the original YMCA and the Converse Hotel. Most of the middle and upper left of this photograph shows the mill district, which is now completely gone. The hydraulic canal, seen across the middle of the photograph, sent water to the mills and the power plant in the gorge. This view has changed dramatically since the time of this photograph.

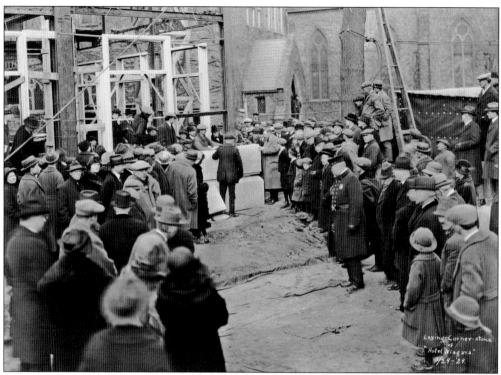

Above, a crowd watches the laying of the cornerstone of the Hotel Niagara in 1924. It was a project of the chamber of commerce, financed by public subscription. It was opened with a formal dinner and ball on April 8, 1925. In the lobby of the new hotel was a huge floral piece with 3,000 white carnations representing North America.

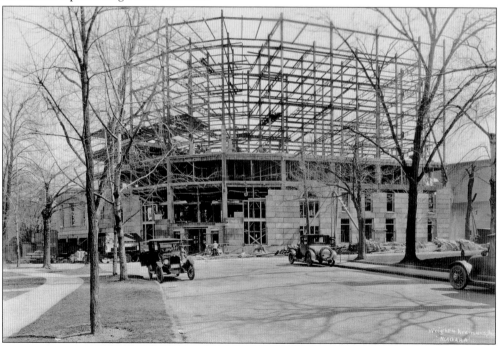

This 1974 photograph shows the Hotel Niagara. In April 1999, *Niagara Gazette* reporter Don Glynn wrote, "The Hotel Niagara was envisioned as a civic, social and commercial center to accommodate every major function in the Cataract City. A short walk from the nation's oldest state park, the 200-room hotel was designed as THE place to stay. Over the years, the ballroom was occupied virtually every day and often at night."

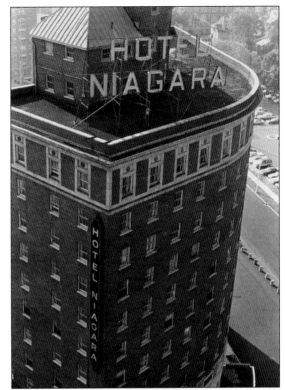

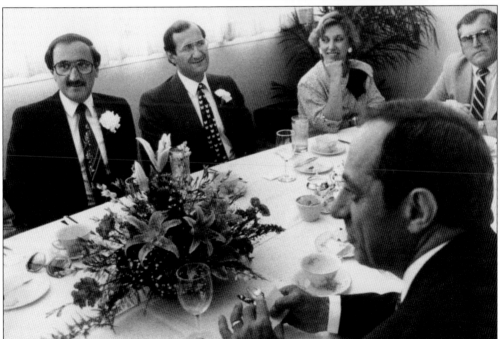

On July 10, 1986, Governor Cuomo addressed Ghermezian brothers Nadar and Raphael about building the Mall of American in downtown Niagara Falls. Failing to develop this idea has long since been noted as one of the major economic disappointments in recent Niagara Falls history.

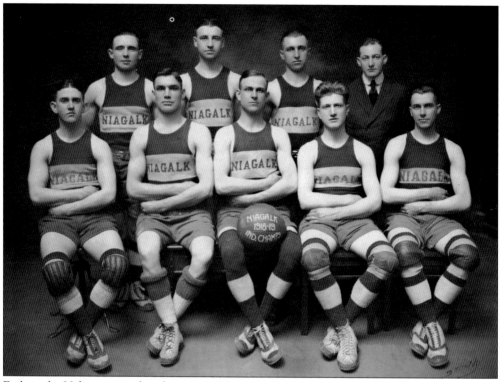

Early in the 20th century, when factories in Niagara Falls were booming with profits and expansions, workers organized into unions and athletic teams. Competition was lively. Here is the Niagara Alkali basketball team of 1918–1919. Niagara Alkali began operations in Niagara Falls in 1901, using the electricity produced there to convert salt into bases. For example, sodium chloride (table salt) was converted into chlorine and sodium hydroxide.

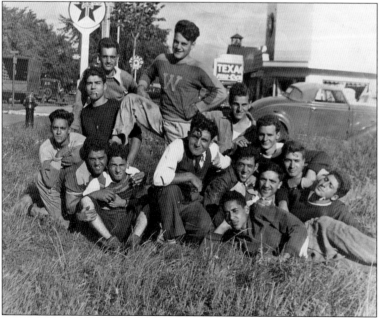

The Mustachio Football Club is seen here in the fall of 1938. Pictured here after a sandlot game are, from left to right, Dominic Paonessa, Roy Corrieri, Al Salacuse, Sam Chirumblo, Gordon Stewart, Guido Virtuoso, Dominic Mitro, Paul Brucato, Domenick Spacone, Connie Manuse, Peter Paonessa, Al Amato, Vic Montani, and Joe Marino.

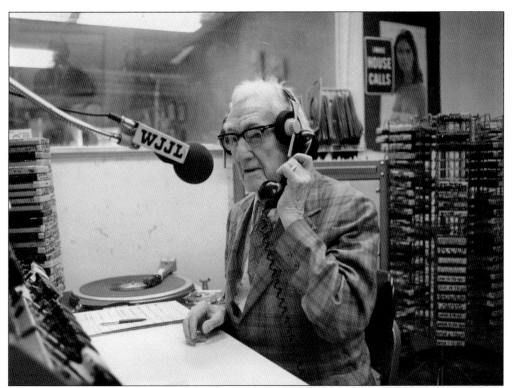

Dr. Edwin Larter is seen hosting the Niagara Falls radio station WJJL's *Viewpoint* telephone call in show, Thursday, December 12, 1974, on his 105th birthday. His subject on this date was the secret to longevity. The *Viewpoint* program has been popular with Niagara Falls residents for many years.

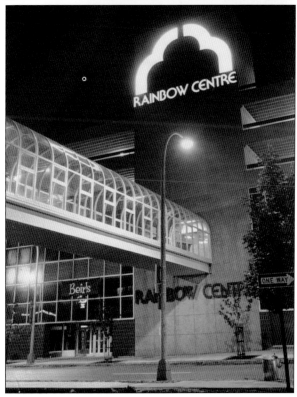

The Rainbow Centre Mall opened on July 2, 1982, as part of a failed urban renewal project. Initially, the mall was successful, but it did not turn a profit until 1990, when the original anchor, Beir's Department Store, was replaced with a Burlington Coat Factory, and the majority of the mall tenants were replaced with outlet stores. It closed September 30, 2000. (Courtesy of the *Niagara Gazette*.)

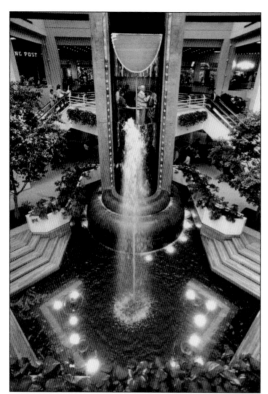

The Rainbow Centre's defining feature was a beautiful fountain near the food court. In the late 1990s, the mall lost its designation as the most successful in Niagara Falls when the Fashion Outlets renovated. The Rainbow Centre was not upgraded after opening and simply could not compete. The mall closed September 30, 2000. (Courtesy of the *Niagara Gazette*.)

Ice skaters enjoy the rink at E. Dent Lackey Plaza around 1988. From 1981 to 2000, Niagara Falls celebrated its 44-day winter Festival of Lights. Costs and low attendance caused the end of this festival. From 1925 to 1930, the city celebrated a Festival of Lights in June for a few days each year. It was so popular that some said it could have reached the status of Mardi Gras or the Tournament of Roses. The Great Depression put an end to the summer festivals. (Courtesy of the *Niagara Gazette*.)

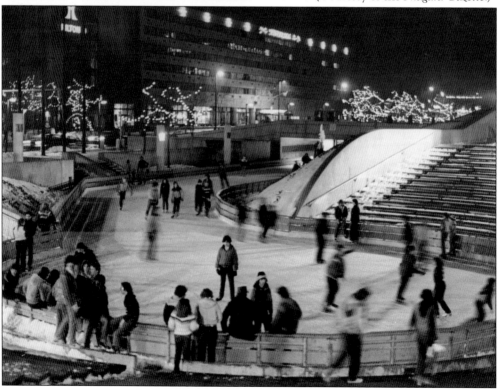

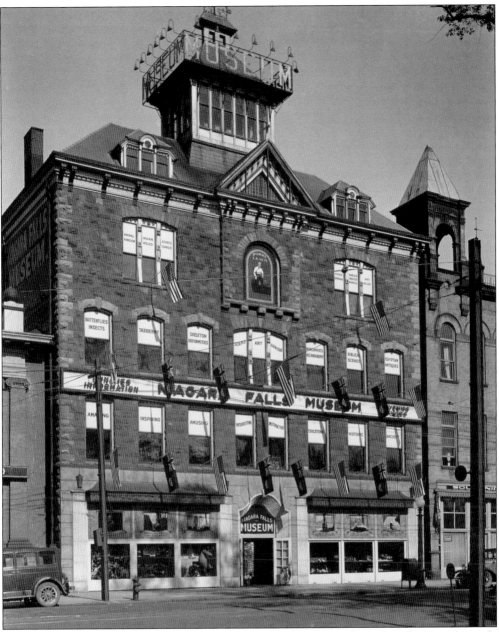

The Niagara Falls Museum was built in 1827 by Thomas Barnett and stood on the Canadian side of the falls. It was relocated and rebuilt several times before relocating to the American side in 1888, where it stood for another 70 years before urban renewal forced the museum to move again, back to Canada. The museum claimed to have over 700,000 exhibits, ranging from Egyptian mummies, mastodon remains, and a humpback whale to a collection of "the most interesting deformities in the world."

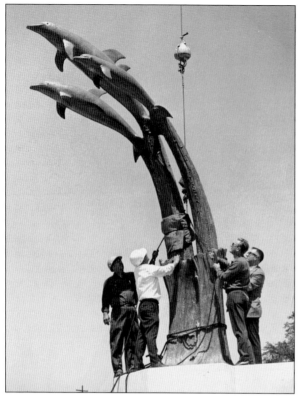

This 1966 photograph shows the Aquarium of Niagara one year after it opened. It has changed its exhibits through the years and remains a popular family attraction. It is located close to the Niagara Gorge Discovery Center between Whirlpool and Third Streets. The Aquarium of Niagara is visited by thousands of residents, tourists, and schoolchildren every year.

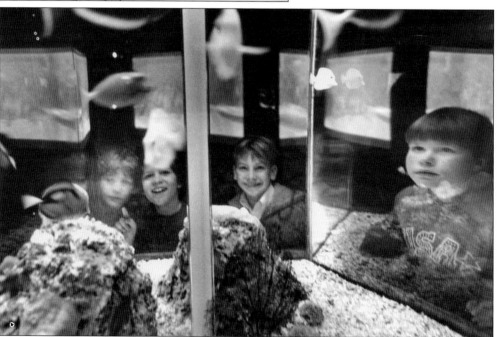

From left to right, Seventy-ninth Street School students David Stott, Brian Lee, Fred Blackwell, and Jason Stumbo stare in awe at the swimming fish while on a field trip to the Aquarium of Niagara in 1984.

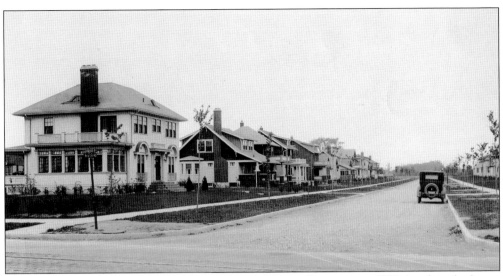

Howard Morley, the manager of the International Paper Company in 1930, lived in the house on the far left corner in this photograph. This house was on River Road (now Buffalo Avenue) and Shepard Avenue (now Sixty-seventh Street) in LaSalle, a village that was annexed to the city of Niagara Falls in 1927. LaSalle is still known today for its picturesque streets and beautiful, tree-lined neighborhoods.

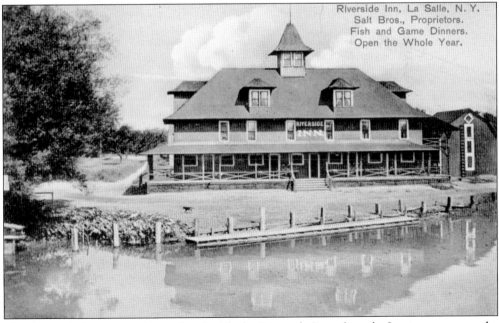

The Riverside Inn, not to be confused with the Riverside Inn of nearby Lewiston, was on the shore of the Little Niagara River around 1907. The Little Niagara River separates Cayuga Island from the mainland. This spacious restaurant and inn advertised their fish and game dinners, served year-round.

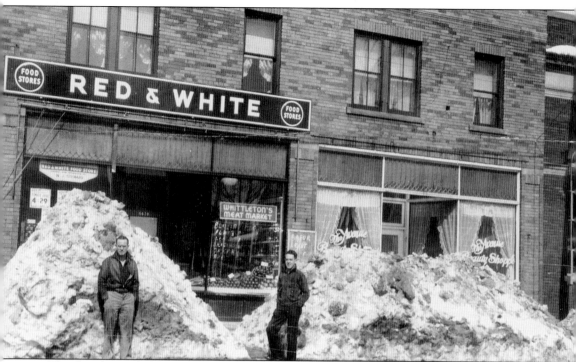

The plows have piled the snow high in front of the Red & White Food Store at 8670 Buffalo Avenue in LaSalle after a winter snowstorm in 1936. Scenes like this one are common in Niagara Falls during the winter months. From left to right are the Red & White Food Store with Whittleton's Meat Market located inside and the Avenue Beauty Shoppe at 8672 Buffalo Avenue. MacLeod's Pharmacy, owned by the Kendzia family, now occupies this site.

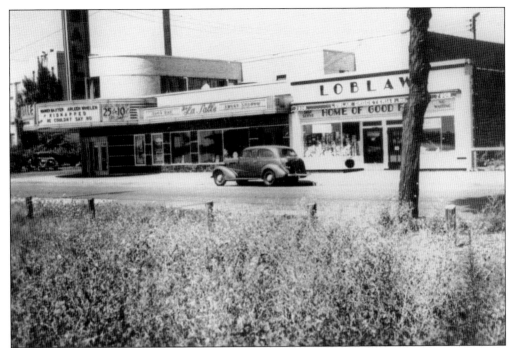

From left to right in this 1938 photograph of LaSalle are the Basil's LaSalle Theater, LaSalle Soda Bar and Sweet Shop, and Loblaws Grocerteria, located at Seventy-sixth Street and Buffalo Avenue. A Wilson Farms convenience store now stands on the corner where Basil's LaSalle Theater once stood.

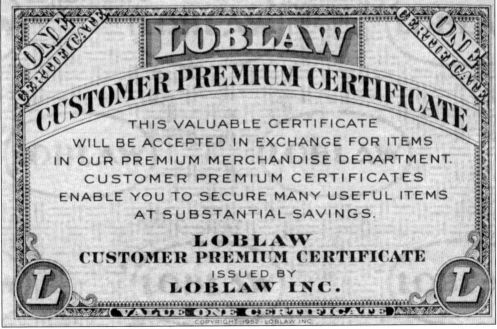

The Loblaw Grocerteria used these certificates to increase sales. The certificates were redeemed for small appliances and other useful household items.

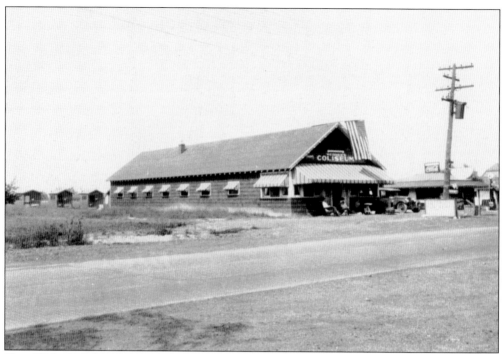

Flora Weber's Coliseum, Cottages, and Restaurant was located on the corner of Cayuga Drive and Ninety-fourth Street around the 1920s. Note the Texaco gas pump in front of the restaurant. During the 1950s and 1960s, the building became Ray Wolney's Delicatessen. Tom Heisner's Trailer Court now stands on the site of the restaurant.

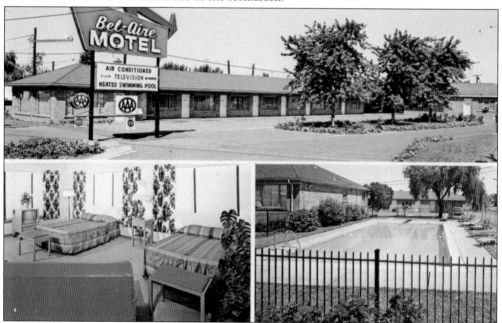

This late 1960s postcard shows the Bel-Aire Motel sign advertising the motel's air-conditioning and color television, along with the heated swimming pool. Many motels like this once populated Route 62, one of the busiest stretches of road in Niagara Falls.

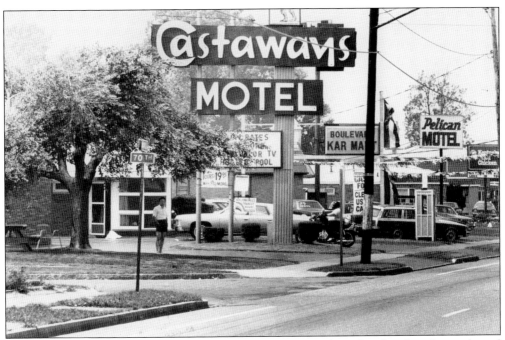

Route 62, also known as Pine Avenue or Niagara Falls Boulevard, is lined with motels and hotels for a few miles heading in and out of the city of Niagara Falls. Vegas-style signs and neon advertising still decorate this stretch of roadway. With the amount of tourists seeking cheap lodging, shopping, and dining during all months of the year, Niagara Falls Boulevard is usually the most traffic-filled street in the city.

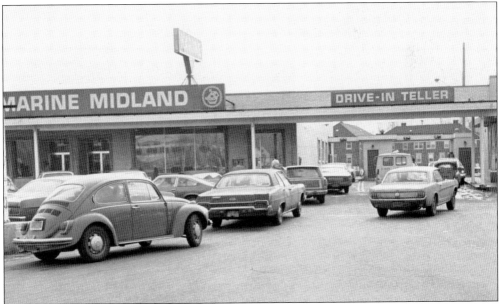

A busy Pine Plaza along Pine Avenue (Niagara Falls Boulevard) is pictured here in 1975. Marine Midland featured drive-through banking right through the middle of the plaza, with cars exiting onto Krull Parkway. The apartment complex, located on Krull Parkway, can be seen in the background to the right.

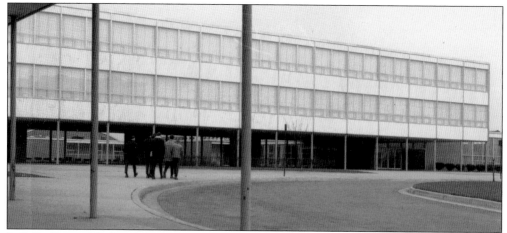

LaSalle Senior High School, pictured here around 1980, opened on March 25, 1957. It was enlarged in 1961 and 1988. Closed in June 2000, it was replaced the following September by a new high school located on Porter Road. Today, there are restaurants and a super Walmart where the school formerly stood.

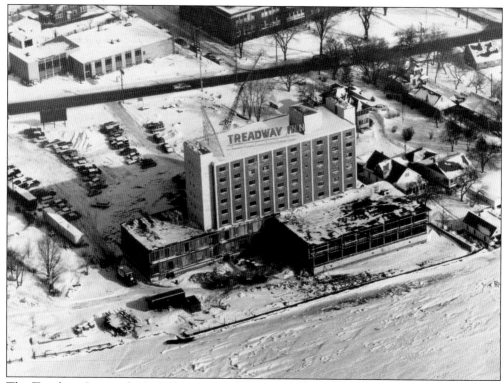

The Treadway Inn in the LaSalle section of Niagara Falls is pictured on a cold winter day in 1963. John F. Kennedy spent part of the day in Niagara County on September 28, 1960, while campaigning for the presidency. He spoke in North Tonawanda, then traveled to Niagara Falls and addressed a crowd in front of the Treadway Inn on Buffalo Avenue. The inn kept busy hosting local events, such as the very popular weekly Iney Wallens radio show, where outstanding citizens were given the Good Neighbor Award and Iney interviewed people from local organizations and famous visitors.

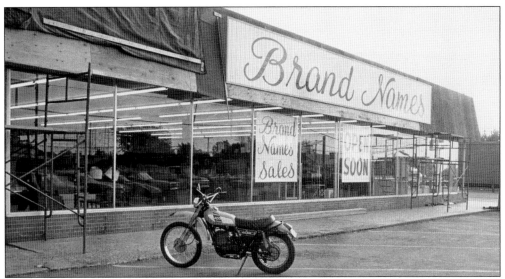

Brand Names catalog store is about to have its grand opening in October 1976. The building once housed the popular Tops Friendly Markets grocery store, before they moved across the street to a larger location.

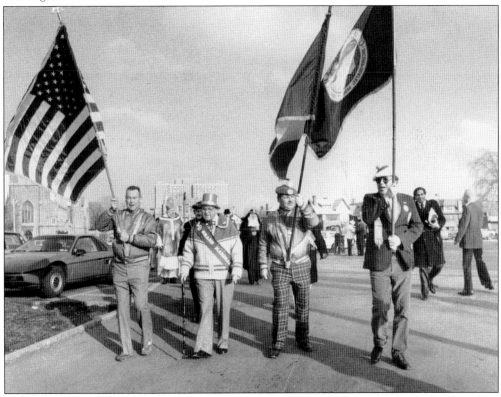

Grand marshal Jimmy Thompson, retired Niagara Falls recreation director, leads the annual St. Patrick's Day Parade on March 17, 1986. This date is also the anniversary of the incorporation of the city of Niagara Falls from the village of Suspension Bridge and the village of Niagara Falls. On June 1, 1927, the village of LaSalle was annexed to the city of Niagara Falls.

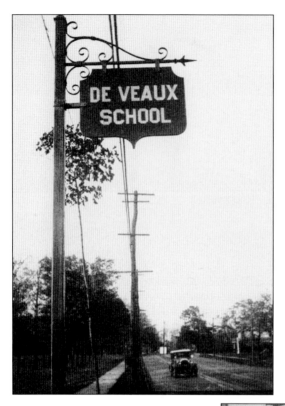

DeVeaux School was established April 15, 1853, as a private school for orphans and destitute children. It was paid for and built on land owned by the late Samuel DeVeaux, who specifically provided for the school in his will. Closed in 1971, its grounds are now DeVeaux Woods State Park, part of which is an old-growth forest. This photograph was taken on Lewiston Road in the early part of the 20th century.

From left to right, Joel and Albert Jaffe and patrolman Anthony Casillo chat on Main Street on April 25, 1982. There were still many stores open on the street at this time. When the villages merged in 1892 to form the city of Niagara Falls, the most-used shopping area in the village to the south (Niagara Falls) became the "South End," and the most-used shopping area in the village to the north (Suspension Bridge) became the "North End."

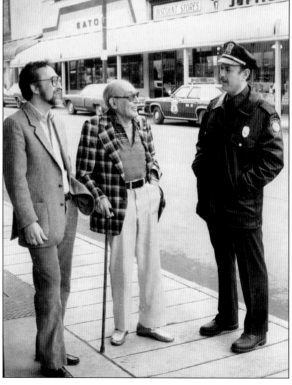

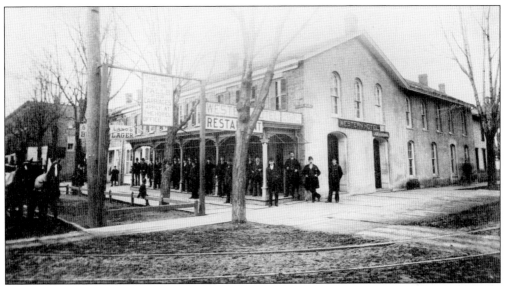

The Western Hotel was located not far from the falls. Note the sign: "This Way to the Falls for Carriages." Also, note the "Lady's Entrance" on the side of the building to the right.

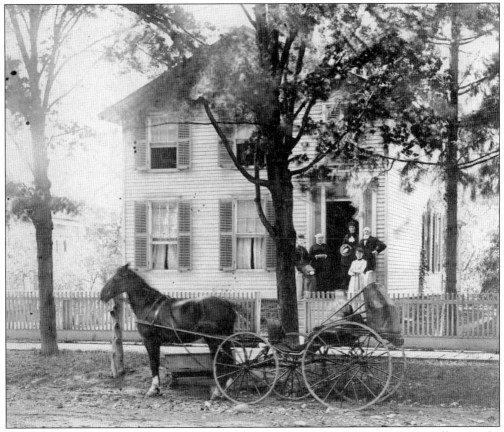

This home was located on Fourth Street in what was once the village of Niagara Falls, near St. Mary's Church. Pictured here in 1870, a horse and buggy is parked in front of the house.

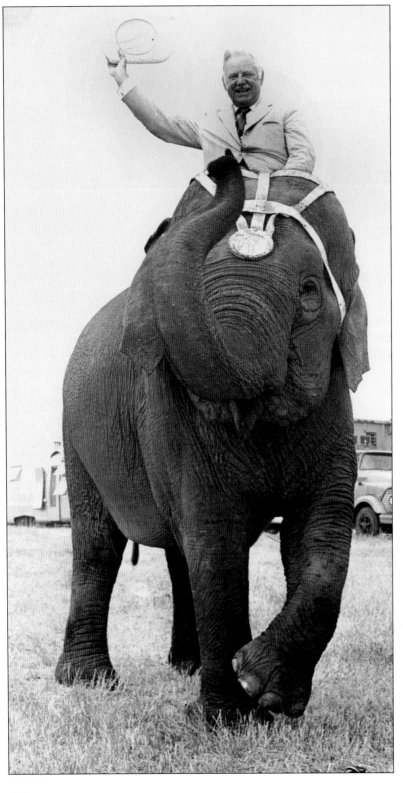

Mayor E. Dent Lackey is still one of the most talked about public figures from the 1960s and 1970s. Lackey was an ex-Methodist minister who decided in the mid-1960s to pursue a political career. The flamboyant and over-the-top Lackey—sometimes riding a white horse at the head of a parade—is still blamed for spearheading an urban renewal policy that eventually led to the destruction of hundreds of historic properties and buildings in order to make way for new and improved stores, shopping centers, and hotels. This dream never materialized and, in fact, has become quite the nightmare for the city's economy. Here, E. Dent Lackey trades in his white horse for an elephant in 1969.

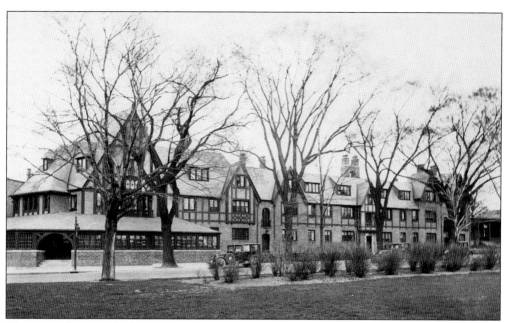

This 1925 photograph shows the Red Coach Inn, built in 1923 by the Schoellkopf family. This distinctive Tudor establishment is named after the red carriage that brought Gen. Marquis de LaFayette to Niagara Falls in 1825. The inn overlooks the American Rapids. LaFayette wanted to purchase Goat Island from the Porters, but they declined his generous offer. Sixty years later, they sold it to the State of New York.

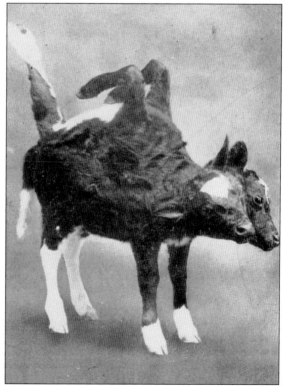

Niagara Falls sometimes attracts strange people with even stranger things or ideas. This poor creature was displayed in the city of Niagara Falls, as seen in this c. 1910 postcard. Noted on the postcard as living on Nineteenth Street, this calf may have found its way into the Niagara Falls Museum into their deformity exhibition at some point. Residents have been known to keep a wide variety of strange animals over the years, including lions and elephants.

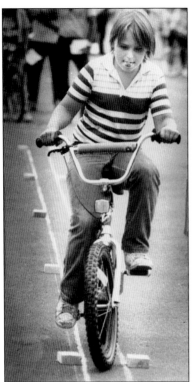

A 12-year-old Billy Rodgers gingerly pedals his way through one of the obstacles set up during the Bicycle Safety Rodeo Tuesday at Goat Island. On June 11, 1986, he was one of several youngsters testing their bicycle skills during the annual event, which is sponsored by the Police Athletic League and the Niagara Frontier State Park Commission.

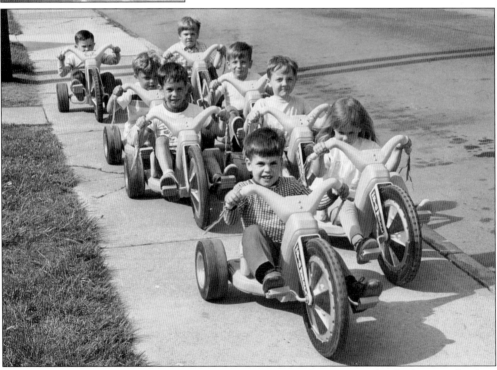

The "Peddle Brigade" cruises down a city street on their Big Wheels during the late summer in 1980.

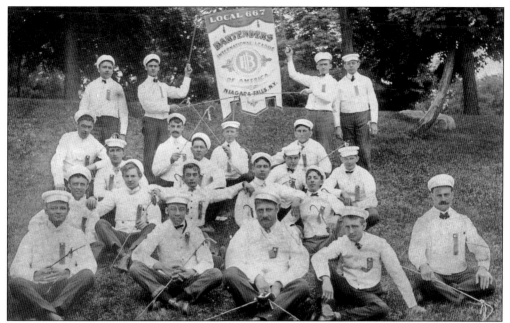

Pictured here around 1901 is the Bartenders International League of America, Local 667 of Niagara Falls, New York. Hotel and restaurant bartenders of the time belonged to a local union in order to make sure working conditions were safe and that every member was able to make a decent living using mixology skills. An offshoot of these unions still exists today.

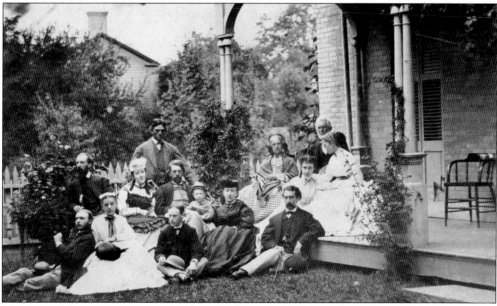

Members of the most prominent family in the history of Niagara Falls gather here in the early 20th century to enjoy a fine summer day. The man with the dark beard on the far left is Alexander Jeffrey Porter. He led a long and distinguished career, serving as treasurer of the Pettebone Paper Company, secretary of the Niagara Falls Power Company, treasurer and later president of the Shredded Wheat Company, director of the Bank of Niagara, and trustee of the Niagara County Savings Bank and the Niagara Falls Memorial Hospital. He died in 1932.

DISCOVER THOUSANDS OF LOCAL HISTORY BOOKS
FEATURING MILLIONS OF VINTAGE IMAGES

Arcadia Publishing, the leading local history publisher in the United States, is committed to making history accessible and meaningful through publishing books that celebrate and preserve the heritage of America's people and places.

Find more books like this at
www.arcadiapublishing.com

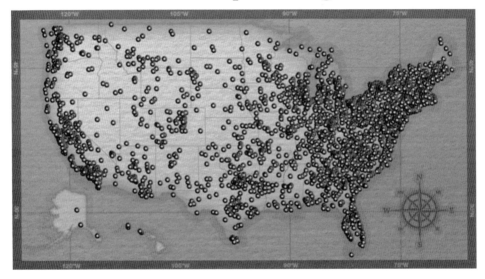

Search for your hometown history, your old stomping grounds, and even your favorite sports team.

Consistent with our mission to preserve history on a local level, this book was printed in South Carolina on American-made paper and manufactured entirely in the United States. Products carrying the accredited Forest Stewardship Council (FSC) label are printed on 100 percent FSC-certified paper.

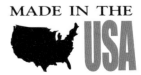

MADE IN THE USA